Amsterdam

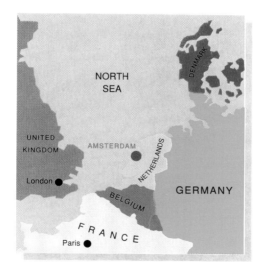

HarperCollins*Publishers*

Your Collins Traveller Guide will help you find your way around your chosen destination quickly and easily. It is colour-coded for easy reference:

The blue section answers the question 'I would like to see or do something; where do I go and what do I see when I get there?' This section is arranged as an alphabetical list of topics. Within each topic you will find:
- A selection of the best examples on offer.
- How to get there, costs and opening hours for each entry.
- The outstanding features of each entry.
- A simplified map, with each entry plotted and the nearest landmark or transport access.

The red section is a lively and informative gazetteer. It offers:
- Essential facts about the main places and cultural items.
  What is La Bastille? Who was Michelangelo? Where is Delphi?

The gold section is full of practical and invaluable travel information. It offers:
- Everything you need to know to help you enjoy yourself and get the most out of your time away, from Accommodation through Baby-sitters, Car Hire, Food, Health, Money, Newspapers, Taxis, Telephones to Youth Hostels.

Cross-references:

Type in small capitals – CHURCHES – tells you that more information on an item is available within the topic on churches.

A-Z after an item tells you that more information is available within the gazetteer. Simply look under the appropriate name.

A name in bold – **Holy Cathedral** – also tells you that more information on an item is available in the gazetteer – again simply look up the name.

CONTENTS

CONTENTS

▓ PRACTICAL INFORMATION GAZETTEER

INTRODUCTION

What is it about Amsterdam that draws over one-and-a-half million
visitors each year, a number which puts it fourth to Rome, London and
Paris in the league of European tourist attractions?

After all, it is in essence a small city, and it is not spectacular, at least
not in the sense of offering sights which impress by their magnificence.
Although the capital of the Netherlands, it lacks the kind of civic
grandeur commonly associated with capital cities, one explanation for
which is the odd fact that the seat of the nation's government is elsewhere, at The Hague. It has few, if any, monuments which can be
described as great. Yet you could not possibly say of Amsterdam (to
adapt Churchill's comment on Clement Attlee) that it is a modest little
place with much to be modest about. Instead you would have to say
that, yes, it is unassuming, its buildings mostly bourgeois in spirit rather
than patrician, its overall character intimate rather than imposing, and
that therein lies a large part of its distinctive charm.

Because Amsterdam does not intimidate, because it is not bewilder-
ingly large, because it does not boast vistas or edifices which overawe,
you feel physically at ease there, with a sense that everything around
you is on a properly human scale. And this feeling of physical ease is
immensely enhanced by the city's most striking topographical feature,
its 160 canals which add up to 100 km of waterways. Amsterdam is
softened and made delightfully picturesque by its canals, as it is by the
tall and graceful trees which stand at intervals along them and the
many small bridges which curve over them.

There is good reason to take to the canals in one of the glass-roofed
boats provided by the several operators of such trips. It is a pleasantly
effortless way to see the handsome mansions and warehouses which
overlook the principal canals, the majority dating from the 17thC and
exemplifying Dutch architecture at its most idiosyncratic and appeal-
ing, particularly in the variety of gables. If you make your canal trip
after dark, you will have a lovely impression of large, lighted windows,
each with enticing hints of civilized living within, shedding a golden
radiance over the black water.

As is true of any city, however, the only way really to get the feel of
Amsterdam is, of course, by discovering it for yourself. The rewards will
be many. Few cities bespeak their history as attractively as Amsterdam,

and in none does contemporary life seem more enjoyable. Amsterdam's history, though not long, is rich with interest. The sophisticated metropolis of today – the second port of the Netherlands as well as the capital and a financial centre of world importance – began life as a fishing settlement established around 1225 on the bank of the river Amstel where it joined the river IJ to flow into the Zuider Zee and thence into the North Sea. Fifty years later the inhabitants of the expanding settlement built a dam on the Amstel, hence the name

'Amstelledamme', which in due course became 'Amsterdam'. From 1300, when it was first granted a city charter, Amsterdam developed into an ever more thriving port and an increasingly prosperous trading city. The peak of its fortunes came in the 17thC when, as the foremost port and chief city of Holland, it was the hub of the vast maritime empire opened up by Dutch merchants (those of the Dutch East India Co., for example, which was founded in 1602) and the mainspring of the nation's emergence as a world power.

It is a paradox that this city, made by merchants and still seeming at first acquaintance quintessentially bourgeois, should have had a long tradition of liberalism. Amsterdammers were noted in the past not only for their religious toleration but for their respect for freedom of conscience in all matters. This cast of mind is manifest today in the tolerance of the majority of Amsterdammers towards the minority who cultivate alternative styles of life. The policy of the city authorities as regards drugs and prostitution can also be seen as characteristically tolerant, although shrewd might be a more apt description – legalizing soft drugs and corralling prostitutes conspicuously in one area are sensible methods of control. The Red-light District of Amsterdam, which is in the *Walletjes*,

the old city centre, provides the now famous spectacle of 'girls' by the hundred brazenly displaying themselves in front rooms which often seem a parody of the bourgeois parlour. The old part of the city also provides, in particular venues, the public performances of live sex which have earned Amsterdam its reputation as a sex capital. The 'live and let live' atmosphere of Amsterdam makes it, in general, a most relaxing place to be in. As you find your way around, you feel not just physically at ease but somehow emotionally at ease as well, untrammelled by convention.

The chances are you will choose to discover the city on foot. Nothing could be more agreeable than strolling beside the Herengracht or the Keizersgracht or the Prinsengracht, the three great semicircular canals which were built in the 17thC and comprise the celebrated *grachtengordel* (canal girdle). Ambling through the area known as the Jordaan is hardly less of a pleasure: once the French sector of Amsterdam and primarily a working-class district, the Jordaan is now the bohemian quarter of the city, an alluring mixture of lively cafés and restaurants, avantgarde galleries and small bookshops, trendy boutiques and hippy-ish arts-and-crafts shops. Alternatively, you may opt for doing your exploring by bicycle. Hiring one is simple and riding one gives you the satis-

fying sensation of being an honorary Amsterdammer (one of many engaging facts about Amsterdam is that it has a bicycle count of 540,000 for a population of 750,000). A bicycle ride or two could take you to the Singel canal to see the floating flower market, to the Amstel to see some of the prettiest of Amsterdam's 2800 houseboats, to the historic square known as the Dam to see the somewhat ponderously Baroque Koninklijk Paleis, to the Anne Frank Huis on Prinsengracht, to Het Rembrandthuis (Rembrandt House) in the old Jewish sector of the city, to Waterlooplein to see the flea market, to the Rijksmuseum to see its magnificent display of paintings by Rembrandt, Vermeer, de Hoogh and other Dutch Masters, to the Van Gogh Museum to see its unparalleled representation of this marvellous artist's work, to the Stedelijk Museum to see its excellent collection of modern and contemporary art, to one of the traditional brown cafés of Amsterdam for a restorative cup of coffee or perhaps a nip of Dutch gin, to … the possibilities in this most seductive of cities seem endless. Whatever the means of transport you decide on, the only thing likely to vex you in Amsterdam is the sheer amount of interesting things to see and pleasurable things to do.

Elizabeth Claridge

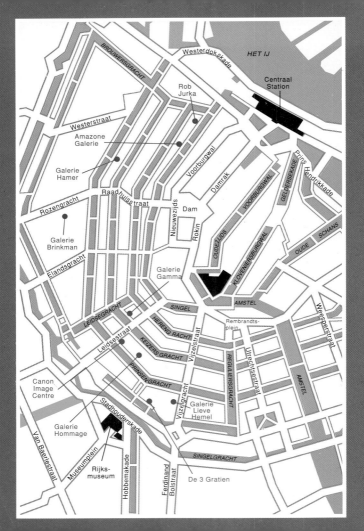

GALERIE GAMMA Keizersgracht 429.
■ 1130-1730 Tue.-Sat. Tram 1, 2, 5. ● Free.
Exhibitions of contemporary art.

GALERIE HAMER Leliegracht 38.
■ 1330-1730 Tue.-Sat. Tram 13, 14, 17. ● Free.
A small gallery specializing in naïve art.

GALERIE LIEVE HEMEL Vijzelgracht 6-8.
■ 1200-1800 Tue.-Sat. Tram 16, 24, 25. ● Free.
Contemporary Dutch realist paintings and sculptures exhibited in an attractive 17thC house with steep staircases and low ceilings.

GALERIE BRINKMAN Rozenstraat 59.
■ Hours vary. Tram 13, 14. ● Free.
Contemporary paintings and objets d'art.

ROB JURKA Singel 28.
■ 1200-1700 Wed.-Sat., 1500-1700 Sun. Tram 1, 2, 5, 13, 17. ● Free.
Contemporary paintings and photographs.

GALERIE HOMMAGE Kerkstraat 142.
■ Hours vary. Tram 1, 2, 5. ● Free.
Contemporary paintings, drawings and prints.

DE 3 GRATIEN Weteringstraat 39.
■ 1200-1730 Tue.-Fri., 1100-1700 Sat. Tram 6, 7, 16, 24, 25. ● Free.
Quite respectable erotic pictures by local artists.

CANON IMAGE CENTRE Leidsestraat 79.
■ 1200-1745 Tue.-Fri., 1100-1645 Sat. Tram 1, 2, 5. ● Free.
International photography. Superb canal views from the upper floors.

AMAZONE GALERIE Singel 72.
■ 1000-1700 Tue.-Fri., 1300-1700 Sat., Sun. Tram 1, 2, 5, 13, 17. ● Free.
Works by female artists and exhibitions on women's issues.

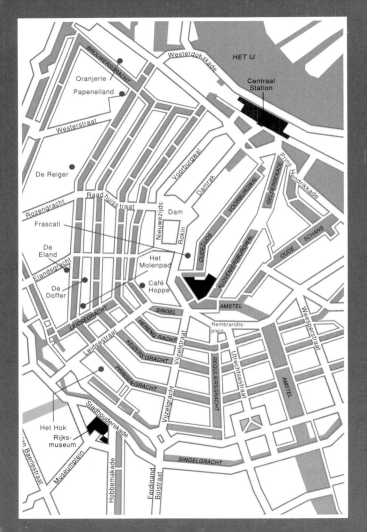

DE DOFFER Runstraat 12. ▓ 1100-0200 Mon.-Thu., 1100-0300 Fri. & Sat., 1200-0200 Sun. Tram 1, 2, 5.
Easy-going little café mostly frequented by students.

FRASCATI Nes 59.
▓ 1000-0100 Mon.-Sat., 1700-0100 Sun. Tram 4, 9, 14, 16, 24, 25.
Elegant décor, reasonably-priced food and a theatre-going clientele.

CAFÉ HOPPE Spui 18.
▓ 0800-0100 Sun.-Thu., 0800-0200 Fri. & Sat. Tram 1, 2, 5.
*Amsterdam's most famous brown café (see **A-Z**) and possibly its busiest. Always buzzing with good-humoured conversation.*

PAPENEILAND Prinsengracht 2. ▓ 1100-0100 Mon.-Thu., 1100-0200 Fri. & Sat., 1400-0100 Sun. Bus 18, 22, 44.
*Notable brown café (see **A-Z**). Atmospheric interior and antique décor.*

ORANJERIE Binnen Oranjestraat 15.
▓ 1100-0100. Tram 3; Bus 18, 22.
Relaxed and friendly atmosphere. Hollywood posters cover the walls.

DE REIGER Nieuwe Leliestraat 34.
▓ 0900-0100 Sun.-Thu., 0900-0200 Fri. & Sat. Tram 13, 14, 17.
*One of the most popular Jordaan (see **A-Z**) cafés.*

DE ELAND Prinsengracht 296.
▓ 1000-0100 Sun.-Thu., 1000-0200 Fri. & Sat. Tram 13, 14, 17.
Captures the atmosphere of old Amsterdam. Terrace overlooking canal.

HET MOLENPAD Prinsengracht 653.
▓ 1200-0100 Sun.-Thu., 1200-0200 Fri. & Sat. Tram 1, 2, 5, 7, 10.
An attractive setting and one of the best café cuisines in the city.

HET HOK Lange Leidsedwarsstraat 134.
▓ 1000-0100 Sun.-Thu., 1000-0200 Fri. & Sat. Tram 1, 2, 5.
Games like chess, draughts and backgammon are a popular feature.

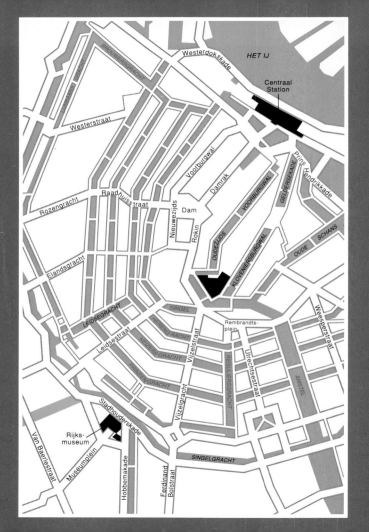

CANALS & RIVERS

AMSTEL RIVER
Tram 6, 7, 9, 10, 14; M Waterlooplein, Weesperplein.
Natural waterway with more open outlook than the canals, featuring the Magere Brug (see A-Z) and the Carré Theatre (see THEATRE & CINEMA 1).

SINGEL
Tram 4, 9, 14, 16, 24, 25 to Muntplein.
Innermost of the grachtengordel (see Canals). Once the city moat, it now houses the Flower Market (see Drijvende Bloemenmarkt). See WALKS 3, 5.

HERENGRACHT
Tram 1, 2, 5 to Koningsplein.
The 'Gentlemen's Canal', containing some of the grandest merchants' houses, especially between Leidsegracht and Vijzelstraat. See WALK 5.

KEIZERSGRACHT
Tram 13, 14, 17 to Westermarkt.
The 'Emperor's Canal', slightly less grand but still featuring an impressive display of façades and gables. See WALK 5.

PRINSENGRACHT
Tram 13, 14, 17 to Westermarkt.
'Prince's Canal', formerly accommodating tradesmen and artisans. Look out for the old warehouses: many are still in use today. See WALKS 1 & 5.

BROUWERSGRACHT
Tram 3; Bus 18, 22, 44 to Haarlemmerplein.
Some of Amsterdam's prettiest canal views are to be seen along here.

LIJNBAANSGRACHT
Tram 3; Bus 18, 22, 44 to Haarlemmerplein.
Admire the beautiful waterside gardens.

REGULIERSGRACHT
Tram 4, 9, 14 to Rembrandtsplein.
Famous for its view of seven canal bridges in a row. See WALK 5.

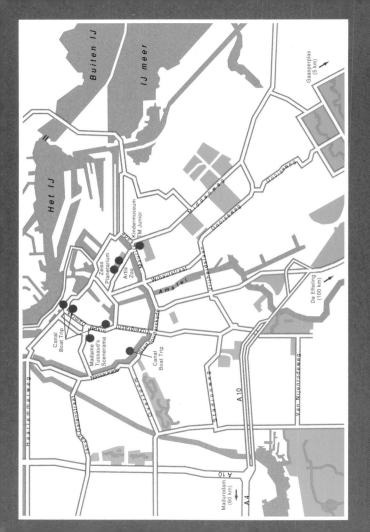

CHILDREN

MADAME TUSSAUD'S SCENERAMA Dam Square 20.
■ 1000-1730. Tram 1, 2, 4, 5, 9, 14, 16, 24, 25. ● f16, child f11.
Exhibits include a re-creation of the Dutch Golden Age and a trip to the moon, with moving figures, and sound, light and special effects.

ARTIS ZOO Plantage Kerklaan 40.
■ 0900-1700. Tram 7, 9, 14; Bus 56. ● f17.50, child f10.
To be congratulated for keeping its animals (some 6000 in all) in conditions closely resembling their natural habitats.

ZEISS PLANETARIUM Plantage Kerklaan 40.
■ 0900-1700. Tram 7, 9, 14; Bus 56.
The universe explained in this planetarium in the zoo (see above).

KINDERMUSEUM TM JUNIOR Linnaeusstraat 2a.
■ Reopens June 1992. Tram 9, 14; Bus 22.
Displays and activities on Third World problems, for children aged 6-12.

GAASPERLAS
■ 0800-dusk. M Gaasperplas; Bus 60, 61, 137, 174.
Barbecues, picnic areas and a water playground. See PARKS.

MADURODAM Haringkade 175, The Hague.
■ 0930-2230 April-June, 0930-2300 July & Aug., 0930-1700 Sep., 0930-1300 Oct. Train or bus to The Hague, then Tram 1, 9.
Miniature town with finely detailed buildings and lots of working models. See A-Z.

DE EFTELING Europaweg 1, Kaatsheuvel.
■ 1000-1800 April-Oct.
Family leisure park with fairy-tale theme and ingenious thrill-rides.

CANAL BOAT TRIP
■ Departures every 15 min. Tram 4, 9, 14, 16, 24, 25. ● f10 per hr.
A 'must' for every visitor. Boarding points on Prins Hendrikkade, Stadhouderskade, Damrak and Rokin. See **Canals**, **Tours & Excursions**.

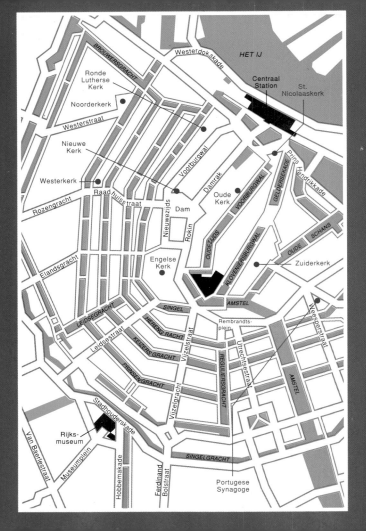

NIEUWE KERK Dam Square.
▦ 1100-1700 Mon.-Sat., 1200-1500 Sun. Closed Jan., Feb. Tram 1, 2, 5.
*Founded in the 15thC and extensively rebuilt since then. It is still used
for State occasions, exhibitions and concerts. See* **WALK 2**.

ENGELSE KERK Begijnhof 48.
Tram 1, 2, 4, 5, 9, 24, 25.
Plain Presbyterian church in a tranquil setting. See **WALK 2**, **Begijnhof**.

OUDE KERK Oudekerksplein 23.
▦ 1000-1600 Mon.-Sat. Tram 4, 9, 16, 24, 25. ● f1.
Amsterdam's biggest church, and its oldest. See **WALK 4**.

WESTERKERK Prinsengracht 281.
▦ 1000-1600 Mon.-Sat. (May-Sep.). Tram 13, 14, 17.
Adorned with an impressive tower offering a splendid view. See **WALK 1**.

NOORDERKERK Noordermarkt.
Tram 3; Bus 18, 22, 44.
Site of Mon. antiques, and Sat. bird and 'organic' markets. See **WALK 1**.

ZUIDERKERK Zuiderkerkhof (enter at St. Antoniesbreestraat 130-2).
▦ 1100-1400 Thu. & Fri., 1100-1600 Sat. (June-Oct.). M Nieuwmarkt.
Amsterdam's first major post-Reformation church.

PORTUGESE SYNAGOGE Jonas Daniël Meijerplein.
Tram 9, 14; Bus 31, 56; M Waterlooplein.
A testimony to the influence of the Jewish community in Amsterdam.

ST. NICOLAASKERK Prins Hendrikkade 73. Opposite Centraal
station. Most trams and buses.
Where Sinterklaas (Santa Claus) begins the Nov. festivities. See **WALK 4**.

RONDE LUTHERSE KERK Singel, at Kattengat. Walking distance
from Centraal station.
Distinctive dome; now a concert and conference venue. See **WALK 5**.

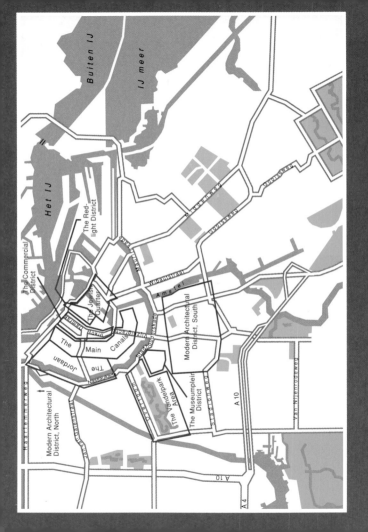

MODERN ARCHITECTURAL DISTRICT, NORTH
Spaarndammerplantsoen, off Zaanstraat. Bus 22, 28.
Three striking housing blocks by Michael de Klerk. See **Architecture**.

THE JORDAAN
Between Prinsengracht and Lijnbaansgracht. Tram 13, 14, 17.
Picturesque jumble of narrow streets, shops and cafés. See WALK 1, **A-Z**.

THE RED-LIGHT DISTRICT
Oudezijds Voorburgwal, Oudezijds Achterburgwal. Tram 4, 9, 16, 24.
Astonishing sights of shamelessly liberal Amsterdam. See WALK 4, **A-Z**.

THE JEWISH QUARTER
Geldersekade to Nieuwe Herengracht. M Nieuwmarkt, Waterlooplein.
Little now remains of Amsterdam's once-thriving Jewish community.

THE COMMERCIAL DISTRICT
Around Nieuwendijk and Kalverstraat. Tram 1, 2, 4, 5, 9, 16, 24, 25.
Characterized by narrow, bustling pedestrianized streets containing all kinds of shops. See SHOPPING 1 & 3.

THE MAIN CANALS
From Brouwersgracht to the Amstel river.
History and commerce intermingle here. Numerous photogenic views.

THE MUSEUMPLEIN DISTRICT
Tram 2, 3, 5, 6, 7, 10, 12.
Cultural heart of Amsterdam, housing the main museums. See SQUARES.

MODERN ARCHITECTURAL DISTRICT, SOUTH
Vrijheidslaan, P. L. Takstraat, J. Vermeerplein, R. Hartplein. Tram 3, 4, 5.
Exceptional housing blocks of the Amsterdam School. See **Architecture**.

THE VONDELPARK AREA
Around Overtoom and Willemsparkweg. Tram 1, 2, 5, 6.
Chic shops and elegant mansions surround the park. See PARKS, **A-Z**.

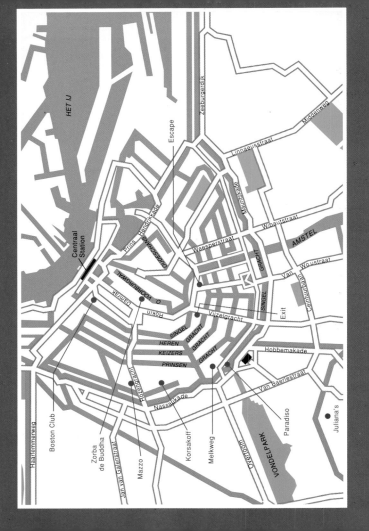

MAZZO Rozengracht 114.
■ 2300-0400 Sun.-Thu., 2300-0500 Fri., Sat. Tram 13, 14. ● f7.50-f10.
Popular with the trendies of the Jordaan (see A-Z).

EXIT Reguliersdwarsstraat 42.
■ 2300-0400 Sun.-Thu., 2300-0500 Fri. & Sat. Tram 16, 24. ● Free.
Same owners as April (see MODERN BARS), a nearby gay bar; always busy.

JULIANA'S Apollolaan 138 (enter on Breitnerstraat).
■ 2200-0400 Sun.-Thu., 2200-0500 Fri. & Sat. Tram 16; Bus 66. ● f5.
Stylish up-market disco in the Hilton Hotel.

BOSTON CLUB Kattengat 1.
■ 2200-0400 Sun.-Thu., 2200-0500 Fri. & Sat. Tram 1, 2, 5, 13. ● Free.
The Ramada Renaissance's superior disco. Expect to pay heavily for drinks.

ZORBA DE BUDDHA Oudezijds Voorburgwal 216.
■ 2100-0200 Sun.-Thu., 2100-0300 Fri. & Sat. Tram 16, 24. ● f5-f10.
Spacious and welcoming disco where drugs are not tolerated. It was established by followers of the Bhagwan Shree Rajneesh.

ESCAPE Rembrandtsplein 11.
■ 2200-0500 Thu.-Sat. Tram 4, 9, 14. ● Free.
Largest disco in town, originally set up to host Sky TV's music shows.

MELKWEG Lijnbaansgracht 234a.
■ 1800-late. Tram 1, 2, 5, 6, 7, 10. ● f5, membership f3.50.
Oddball disco in famous multifunction arts centre. Dancing starts 0100.

PARADISO Weteringschans 6-8.
■ Hours vary; check press for details. Tram 1, 2, 5, 6, 7, 10. ● f5-f10.
Another multipurpose venue, this one located in a converted church.

KORSAKOFF Lijnbaansgracht 161.
■ 2300-0200. Tram 1, 2, 5, 6, 7, 10. ● Free.
Hot and sweaty hangout of cutting-edge nightcrawlers.

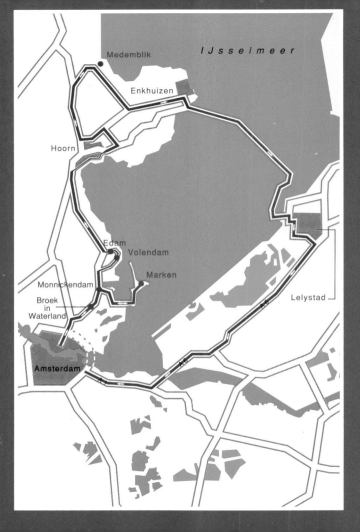

The Old Zuider Zee

A one-day excursion exploring the coastal towns to the north of Amsterdam and the reclaimed polders of Flevoland.

Leave Amsterdam by the IJ Tunnel and head north on the N 10 motorway for 6 km before turning right onto the N 247.

10 km – Broek in Waterland. A pretty and peaceful village with tiny, neat wooden houses dating from the 17th and 18thC. Everything about the place is proudly maintained in a clean and orderly fashion by the inhabitants. Buildings, gardens, streets, pavements – all are immaculate. Continue on the same road.

13 km – Monnickendam. You are now at the former Zuider Zee (see **IJsselmeer, Markermeer**), and the first of a number of fishing villages visited on this excursion. Smoked eel is a favourite delicacy around here, and smokehouses are still in production in the harbour area. Drive 7 km to the east and cross the causeway.

20 km – Marken (see **A-Z**). A trip to this little island is very worthwhile. Many of the locals still wear colourful traditional costumes, adding to the picturesque appeal of the tiny wooden houses. The museum gives an insight into the island's history, and the church contains model fishing boats. Retrace your route to the N 247 at Monnickendam, turn right and head north for 5 km.

32 km – Volendam (see **A-Z**). Sadly the tourist trade has rather spoilt this once much-admired coastal town, but some of the buildings retain their charm. Carry on for 1 km to the north.

33 km – Edam (see **A-Z**). The town which gave its name to the famous cheese has greater appeal than Volendam. The Kaasmarkt (Cheese Market) is an obvious attraction, but also try to make time to explore the Edams Museum at Damplein 8, which contains many fascinating curios (1000-1630 Mon.-Sat., 1330-1630 Sun., April-Oct.). Keep going north along the N 247.

50 km – Hoorn. The town gave its name to Cape Horn, which was first rounded by Willem Schouten, a native of the town, in 1616. Two other well-known citizens who were explorers and colonizers in the 17thC were Jan Pieterszoon Coen, who founded Batavia (now Jakarta), and Abel Tasman, who discovered New Zealand. The attractive waterways and buildings of Hoorn are pleasant to explore, and the Westfries

Museum at Rodesteen 1 has many interesting exhibits, although the lack of explanatory labelling may disappoint the visitor (1100-1700 Mon.-Fri., 1400-1700 Sat. & Sun.). Head inland and northwards on the A 7 and turn right after 12 km, following the signs for Medemblik.

64 km – Medemblik. The town features a busy harbour filled with countless yachts. The Kasteel Radbout beside the harbour stands on the site of a Frisian castle originally dating from the 8thC, and fortified in the 13thC. The nearby twin villages of Twisk and Opperdoes are extremely picturesque. Continue in an easterly direction along the geometric array of polderland roads and you will find yourself passing through many more such attractive communities.

84 km – Enkhuizen (see **A-Z**). One of the highlights of the trip is the Zuider Zee Museum, a fascinating local history museum. The major attraction – a re-creation of a typical Zuider Zee village – is outdoors and only accessible by a special ferry. Allow plenty of time for this excellent museum before enjoying one of those experiences almost unique to the Netherlands – a drive across the sea. The new dyke road will carry you the 30 km over the former Zuider Zee to Flevoland.

114 km – Lelystad. A new town contrasting sharply with the historic towns you have just travelled through. Since the mid-1960s Lelystad has grown from nothing to a settlement of 55,000 inhabitants. It is a fairly dreary place, but its interest lies in the amazing engineering feat that reclaimed all the surrounding land from the sea. Follow the A 6 and then the A 1 motorways back to Amsterdam (50 km) past acres of rapeseed fields, which are a brilliant yellow in the springtime.

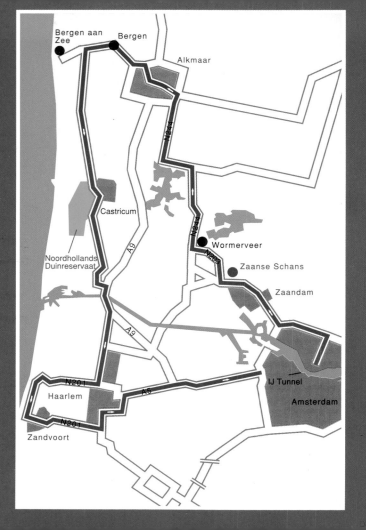

EXCURSION 2

Noord-Holland

A 6 hr excursion visiting the major attractions of Noord-Holland.

Either head north from the city centre through the IJ Tunnel or take the Coentunnel to the west of the city. Turn left, following the signs for Zaandam.

10 km – Zaandam (see **A-Z**). Zaandam and the surrounding towns more or less constitute a sprawling industrial suburb of Amsterdam, but the area is not without its attractions. The Russian tsar, Peter the Great, visited Zaandam several times between 1697 and 1717 to study Dutch shipbuilding techniques. The modest house where he stayed is situated near the Dam and has been converted into a museum. Continue north along the N 203 trunk road for a short distance before turning off to Zaanse Schans.

12 km – Zaanse Schans (see **A-Z**). This pleasant windmill village, constructed in 17thC style, was opened in 1960. The houses, museums and craft shops give you a real taste of life in bygone times. Rejoin the N 203 going north and look out for the N 244 turn-off just after Wormerveer.

30 km – Alkmaar (see **A-Z**). The famous cheese-making centre. If you leave Amsterdam early enough on Fri., you can catch the bustle of the Cheese Market in action before it closes at 1200. Take the westerly road through Bergen and turn left before Bergen aan Zee.

55 km – Noordhollands Duinreservaat. This protected area of forestry and sand dunes lies to your right as you pass Castricum. Go south from here along the A 9 and A 208 motorways.

65 km – Haarlem (see **A-Z**). The capital of the province of Noord-Holland. Recommended sights include the Franz Hals Museum and the Sint Bavokerk (also known simply as the Grote Kerk), but the numerous little backstreets contain enough quaint shops and picturesque courtyards to make a visit enjoyable just by strolling around. On leaving the town, follow the N 201.

75 km – Zandvoort (see **A-Z**). A popular seaside resort with a long sandy beach and all the amenities you would normally expect, including restaurants, cafés, a dolphinarium and a casino. Return to Amsterdam (approximately 30 km) along the N 201 and the A 5 going in an easterly direction.

Tulip Country

A 4 hr excursion to the bulb fields southwest of Amsterdam. Start out early to reach Aalsmeer in time for the flower auction.

Take the A 10 and A 4 motorways out of Amsterdam to just past Schiphol (see **Airport**).
16 km – Aalsmeer (see **A-Z**). The wonderful flower auction is a 'must', so try to reach it well before 0900 or you will miss much of the fun. Flowers may remind you of romance, but the mechanized techniques and businesslike atmosphere here will remind you just how important the trade is to the economy of the Netherlands. Leaving Aalsmeer, follow the westbound N 201.
30 km – Heemstede. This suburb of Haarlem (see **A-Z**) provides an interesting distraction from the tulip fields in the form of the Croquius Expo at Croquiusdijk 27, a fascinating exhibition of old land-reclamation techniques. The N 208 leading south from the town will take you through the *bloembollenstreek*, the main area for bulb cultivation in the Netherlands. During April and May you can enjoy the sight of quite breathtaking expanses of colour.
38 km – Hillegom. This, along with the following two destinations, is one of the main centres for tulip growing. Here you can admire the demonstration garden at Treslong, which contains a quite astonishing number of bulb varieties. Continue along the same road for a further 4 km.
42 km – Lisse. Home of the famous Keukenhof Exhibition (0800-1930 April & May), an immense, spectacular garden with acres of flowerbeds (see **Tulips**) and greenhouses crammed full with wide-ranging displays of flowers and shrubs. An annual flower parade is held in the town at the end of April. For background information on bulb cultivation, visit the museum at Heereweg 219.
46 km – Sassenheim. This town marks the southernmost edge of the tulip country, and from here you can return quickly to Amsterdam on the A 44 and A 4 motorways. Alternatively you could make your way back to the city in a more leisurely fashion along the network of narrow roads which crisscross the bulb fields.

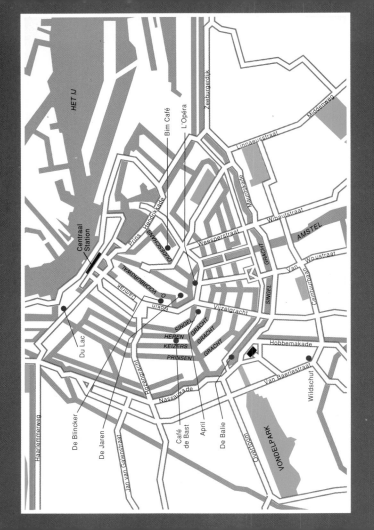

DE BLINCKER St. Barberenstraat 7.
■ 1000-0100. Tram 4, 9, 14, 16, 24, 25.
Split-level interior and ultra-modern décor. Late in the evening it's packed with theatre-goers from the adjacent Frascati Theatre.

DE JAREN Nieuwe Doelenstraat.
■ 1000-0100 Sun.-Thu., 1000-0200 Fri. & Sat. Tram 1, 2, 5.
Elegant 'grand café' with quayside drinking and no-smoking section.

L'OPÉRA Rembrandtsplein, at Bakkersstraat.
■ 1300-0100 Mon.-Thu., 1300-0200 Fri. & Sat. Tram 4, 9, 14.
Decorated in the style of a Parisian brasserie of the 1930s.

APRIL Reguliersdwarsstraat 37.
■ 1400-0100 Sun.-Thu., 1400-0200 Fri. & Sat. Tram 1, 2, 5.
Gay bar, busy in the evenings but retaining a relaxed atmosphere.

CAFÉ DE BAST Huidenstraat 19.
■ 1130-2030 Mon.-Sat., 1700-2030 Sun. Tram 1, 2, 5.
Smart pine décor and a moderately-priced menu.

DU LAC Haarlemmerstraat 118.
■ 1600-0100 Sun.-Thu., 1600-0200 Fri. & Sat. Bus 18, 22.
Has indescribable décor and an extensive kitchen.

BIM CAFÉ Oudeschans 73-79.
■ 2000-0200 Mon.-Thu., 2000-0300 Fri. & Sat. Tram 9, 14.
Situated in the Bimhuis Jazz Centre.

WILDSCHUT Roelof Hartplein 1.
■ 0900-0100. Tram 3, 5, 12, 24.
Art Deco cinema fittings create a pleasant atmosphere.

DE BALIE Kleine-Gartmanplantsoen 10.
■ 1100-0100 Sun.-Thu., 1100-0200 Fri. & Sat. Tram 1, 2, 5, 6, 7, 10.
*Two-storey theatre café, just a stone's throw from Leidseplein (see **A-Z**).*

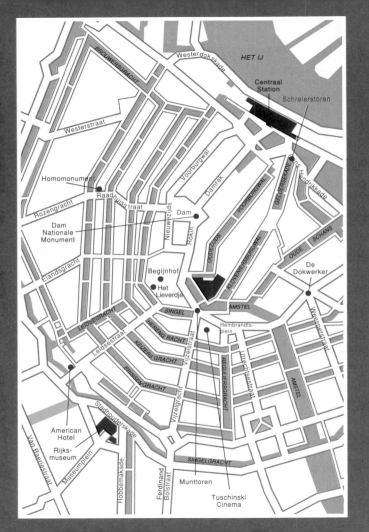

DAM NATIONALE MONUMENT Dam Square.
Tram 4, 9, 16, 24, 25.
Memorial to the dead of World War II. See WALK 2, **Dam Square**.

MUNTTOREN Muntplein.
Tram 4, 9, 14, 16, 24, 25.
Old Mint, built in 1622 on site of one of the city's oldest gates. See **A-Z**.

HET LIEVERDJE Spui.
Tram 1, 2, 5.
Statue of a street urchin, a rallying point for 1960s radicals. See WALK 3.

AMERICAN HOTEL Leidsekade 97.
Tram 1, 2, 5, 6, 7, 10.
Protected building is a long-standing favourite with writers and artists.

TUSCHINSKI CINEMA Reguliersbreestraat 26.
Tram 4, 9, 14, 16, 24, 25.
A fantastic building with remarkable interiors dating from 1921. Cinema 1 is the most ornate. See THEATRE & CINEMA 1, WALK 5.

HOMOMONUMENT Westermarkt.
Tram 13, 14, 17; Bus 21, 67.
Dedicated in 1985 to homosexuals who suffered under the Nazis.

BEGIJNHOF Spui.
Tram 4, 9, 14, 16, 24, 25.
Quiet courtyard in a protected Beguine convent. See WALKS 2 & 3, **A-Z**.

SCHREIERSTOREN Geldersekade. Walking distance from Centraal station. Most trams and buses.
Legendary site of tearful farewells in medieval times. See WALK 4, **A-Z**.

DE DOKWERKER Jonas Daniël Meijerplein.
Tram 9, 14; Bus 31, 56; M Waterlooplein.
Commemorates 1941 dockworkers' strike in support of oppressed Jews.

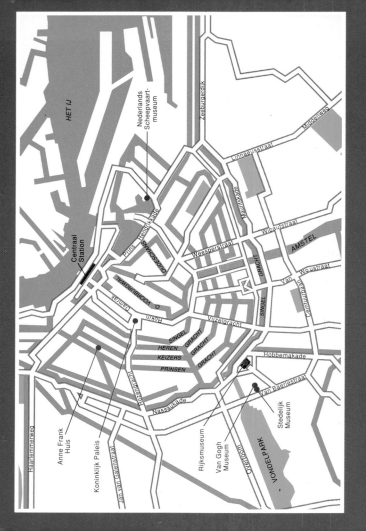

RIJKSMUSEUM Stadhouderskade 42.
▨ 1000-1700 Tue.-Sat., 1300-1700 Sun. Tram 3, 5, 6, 7, 10; Bus 26, 65, 66, 170, 179. ● f6.50 or Museumcard.
Internationally renowned. The Netherlands' major museum of art, housing works by all the great masters of the Golden Age. Also has an excellent collection of foreign schools (French, Flemish, Italian) and Asian art. See **WALK 3**, **A-Z**.

VAN GOGH MUSEUM Paulus Potterstraat 7.
▨ 1000-1700 Tue.-Sat., 1300-1700 Sun. Tram 2, 3, 5, 12, 16; Bus 26, 65, 66, 170, 179. ● f10 or Museumcard.
Offers an insight into the great Dutch artist and his contemporaries through letters and documents, paintings and drawings. See **WALK 3**, **A-Z**.

STEDELIJK MUSEUM Paulus Potterstraat 13.
▨ 1100-1700. Tram 2, 3, 5, 12, 16; Bus 26, 65, 66, 170, 179. ● f7 or Museumcard.
Modern and contemporary paintings, sculpture and photographs. See **WALK 3**, **A-Z**.

ANNE FRANK HUIS Prinsengracht 263.
▨ 0900-1700 Mon.-Sat., 1000-1700 Sun. Tram 13, 14, 17. ● f6.
Concealed behind a sliding bookcase is the attic where Anne wrote her diary as she and her family hid from the Nazis. See **WALKS 1 & 5**, **Frank**.

KONINKLIJK PALEIS (ROYAL PALACE) Dam Square.
▨ 1230-1600 June-Aug. Tram 1, 2, 4, 5, 9, 13, 14, 16, 17, 24, 25. ● f1.
Attractions include opulent interiors and Louis Napoleon's private collection of furnishings. See **OFFICIAL BUILDINGS**, **WALK 2**, **A-Z**.

NEDERLANDS SCHEEPVAARTMUSEUM Kattenburgerplein 1.
▨ 1000-1700 Tue.-Sat., 1300-1700 Sun. Bus 22, 28. ● f10 or Museumcard.
The maritime museum provides an impressive presentation of Dutch naval history in a building which formerly served as the Admiralty arsenal. Magnificently preserved sailing ships are in the harbour.

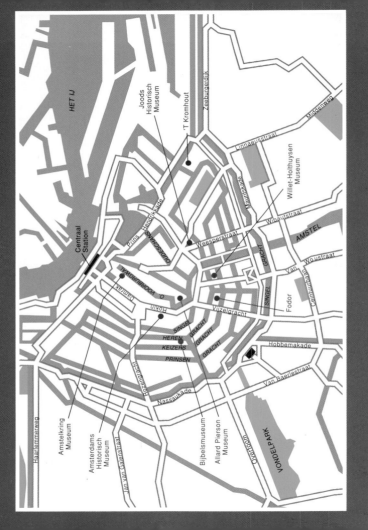

MUSEUMS 2

AMSTERDAMS HISTORISCH MUSEUM Kalverstraat 92.
■ 1100-1700. Tram 1, 2. ● f5 or Museumcard.
Exhibits reflecting the social, commercial and political history of the city.

WILLET-HOLTHUYSEN MUSEUM Herengracht 605.
■ 1100-1700. Tram 4, 9. ● f2.50 or Museumcard.
Evocative re-creation of the interior of a typical 17th-18thC canal house.

ALLARD PIERSON MUSEUM Oude Turfmarkt 127. ■ 1000-
1700 Tue.-Fri., 1300-1700 Sat. & Sun. Tram 4, 9, 14, 16, 24. ● f3.
Archaeological finds from ancient Egypt and the classical world.

BIJBELSMUSEUM Herengracht 366.
■ 1000-1700 Tue.-Sat., 1300-1700 Sun. Tram 1, 2. ● f3 or Museumcard.
Interesting displays on the Bible and its history, in a superb 17thC house.
See **WALKS 3 & 5**.

JOODS HISTORISCH MUSEUM Jonas Daniël Meijerplein 2-4.
■ 1100-1700. Tram 9; M Waterlooplein. ● f7 or Museumcard.
Jewish history and art in Dutch society from the 16thC onwards.

'T KROMHOUT Hoogte Kadijk 147.
■ 1000-1600 Mon.-Fri. Bus 18, 22. ● f2.50.
A former shipyard which escaped closure and demolition in 1970 by conversion into a museum-cum-repair yard.

AMSTELKRING MUSEUM Oudezijds Voorburgwal 40.
■ 1000-1700 Mon.-Sat., 1300-1700 Sun. Tram 4, 9, 16, 24, 25.
● f3.50 or Museumcard.
Known as 'Our Dear Lord in the Attic', this was formerly a secret place of worship for Catholics. Well worth visiting. See **WALK 4**.

FODOR Keizersgracht 609.
■ 1100-1700. Tram 16, 24, 25. ● Admission varies with exhibitions;
Museumcard accepted.
Exhibitions of modern works of art, mainly by Dutch artists.

NEDERLANDS THEATER INSTITUUT Herengracht 168.
▓ 1100-1700 Tue.-Sun. Tram 13, 14, 17. ● f2.50 or Museumcard.
The history of the theatre, including reconstructions of stage sets.

NEDERLANDS FILMMUSEUM Vondelpark 3.
▓ Hours vary – see programme. Tram 1, 2, 3, 5, 6.
● f2.50 or Museumcard.
Ephemera, documents and equipment reflecting cinema history.

HET REMBRANDTHUIS Jodenbreestraat 4-6.
▓ 1000-1700 Mon.-Sat., 1300-1700 Sun. Tram 9. ● f4 or Museumcard.
*250 sketches and etchings by Rembrandt (see A-Z) displayed in the
house where he lived during the 1640s and 1650s.*

NINT TECHNOLOGIE MUSEUM Tolstraat 129.
▓ 1000-1700 Mon.-Fri., 1200-1700 Sat. & Sun. Tram 4. ● f7.
Working machines and models which make science and technology fun.

TROPENMUSEUM Linnaeusstraat 2.
▓ 1000-1700 Mon.-Fri., 1200-1700 Sat. & Sun. Tram 9.
● f6 or Museumcard.
*Aspects of Third World life, especially in former Dutch colonies such as
Indonesia. Next door is the Kindermuseum TM Junior (see CHILDREN).*

HORTUS BOTANICUS Plantage Middenlaan 2.
▓ 0900-1600 Mon.-Fri., 1100-1600 Sat. & Sun. Tram 9, 14. ● f3.
A wide variety of exotic tropical plants.

AVIODOME Schiphol Airport.
▓ 1000-1700 Tue.-Sun. (Nov.-Mar.). Train or bus to Schiphol. ● f6.
The role of the Netherlands in aviation history, with aircraft exhibits.

SIX COLLECTION Amstel 218.
▓ 1000 & 1100 Mon., Wed. & Fri. Tram 4, 9, 14. ● Free admission slip
from Rijksmuseum.
A fine collection of Dutch Old Masters.

SCHRIFTMUSEUM University Library, Singel 425.
■ 0930-1300, 1400-1630 Mon.-Fri. Tram 1, 2, 5. ● Free.
The evolution of handwriting through the ages, from ancient clay tablets to contemporary letters.

GEMEENTEARCHIEF Amsteldijk 67.
■ 0845-1645 Mon.-Fri., 0900-1215 Sat. Tram 3, 4. ● Free.
Amsterdam's municipal archives. On display are posters, photographs and ephemera concerned with the history of the city.

GEOLOGISCH MUSEUM Nieuwe Prinsengracht 130.
■ 0900-1700 Mon.-Fri. Tram 6, 7, 9, 10. ● f3 or Museumcard.
Minerals, ores and fossils from various countries around the world. Largely of specialist appeal.

STICHTING VAN LOON Keizersgracht 672.
■ 1000-1700 Mon., 1300-1700 Sun. Tram 16, 24, 25. ● f5.
House museum containing the Van Loon family's interesting collection of paintings and objets d'art.

SPAARPOTTENMUSEUM Raadhuisstraat 20.
■ 1300-1600 Mon.-Fri. Tram 13, 14, 17. ● f1.50 or Museumcard.
A highly unusual museum (ideal for children) exhibiting a remarkable collection of money boxes – 12,000 in all! See **WALK 2**.

MULTATULI MUSEUM Korsjespoortsteeg 20.
■ 1000-1700 Tue. (other days by appointment only). Tram 1, 2, 5.
● Free.
Small but fascinating museum concerned with the Dutch author who attacked the colonial bourgeoisie of the 19thC.

VERZETSMUSEUM Lekstraat 63.
■ 1000-1700 Tue.-Fri., 1300-1700 Sat. & Sun. Tram 4, 12, 25.
● f5 or Museumcard.
The history of the Dutch Resistance during World War II. An imaginative evocation of the atmosphere of the time.

HOOFPOSTKANTOOR (POST OFFICE) Singel 250. ■ 0830-1800 Mon.-Fri. (2030 Thu.), 0900-1200 Sat. Tram 1, 2, 5, 13, 17.
Recently moved here from P. J. H. Cuypers' remarkable turreted building of 1908 in Nieuwezijds Voorburgwal. See **Architecture***.*

BEURS (STOCK EXCHANGE) Beursplein, off Damrak.
Tram 4, 9, 16, 24, 25.
Designed by the influential architect Hendrik P. Berlage. Nowadays stages occasional exhibitions and recitals. See WALK 2, **Architecture***.*

CENTRAAL STATION Stationsplein. Most trams and buses.
Another grandiose design by Cuypers. Constructed in the late 19thC on an artificial island. See WALKS 2 & 4, **Architecture***.*

STADHUIS/MUZIEKTHEATER Amstel 1.
Tram 9, 14; M Waterlooplein.
New city hall and opera house complex on the site of the old Waterlooplein flea market. See THEATRE & CINEMA 1*.*

RAI Europaplein.
Tram 4; Bus 8, 15, 60.
One of the biggest exhibition and conference centres in the world.

KONINKLIJK CONCERTGEBOUW Van Baerlestraat 98.
Tram 3, 5, 12, 16.
Magnificent acoustics contribute greatly to the worldwide reputation for excellence enjoyed by this concert hall. See THEATRE & CINEMA 1, A-Z*.*

KONINKLIJK PALEIS (ROYAL PALACE) Dam Square.
■ 1230-1600 June-Aug. Tram 1, 2, 4, 5, 9, 13, 14, 16, 17, 24, 25. ● f1.
Built in the 17thC as the town hall, and converted into a palace in 1808 by Louis Napoleon. See MUSEUMS 1, WALK 2, A-Z*.*

BIBLIOTHEEK (MUNICIPAL LIBRARY) Roelof Hartplein 6.
Tram 3, 5, 12.
A fine example of the style of the Amsterdam School (see **Architecture***).*

VONDELPARK Stadhouderskade.
■ 0800-dusk. Tram 1, 2, 3, 5, 6, 12.
The city's most central large park, famous for hippy happenings in the 1960s. 120 acres of lawns, flowerbeds, lakes. See CITY DISTRICTS, **A-Z**.

AMSTELPARK Europaboulevard.
■ 0800-dusk. Bus 8, 49, 60, 157, 173.
Attractions include a maze, an attractive garden and a miniature railway.

AMSTERDAMSE BOS Amstelveenseweg.
■ 0800-dusk. Bus 170, 171, 172.
The largest park in Amsterdam, with facilities for horse riding, cycling, water sports, tennis, picnicking and camping (see **A-Z**). *See* **Nature**.

GAASPERPLAS
■ 0800-dusk. M Gaasperplas; Bus 60, 61, 137, 174.
Water playground with sporting facilities and amenities for barbecues and camping (see **A-Z**). *See* CHILDREN.

SARPHATIPARK Ceintuurbaan.
■ 0800-dusk. Tram 3.
A small, pretty park with well-tended flowerbeds and pleasant aspects. Situated in the Old South.

OOSTERPARK Linnaeusstraat.
■ 0800-dusk. Tram 3, 6, 9, 14.
A restful spot, convenient for the Tropenmuseum (see MUSEUMS 3*).*

BEATRIXPARK Diepenbrockstraat.
■ 0800-dusk. Tram 4; Bus 60, 85, 87.
A pleasant area with ponds and waterways situated close to the RAI (see OFFICIAL BUILDINGS) *and the 1933 Remonstrants church.*

REMBRANDTPARK Postjesweg.
■ 0800-dusk. Bus 18, 19, 64.
Extensive park with large artificial lakes and waterways.

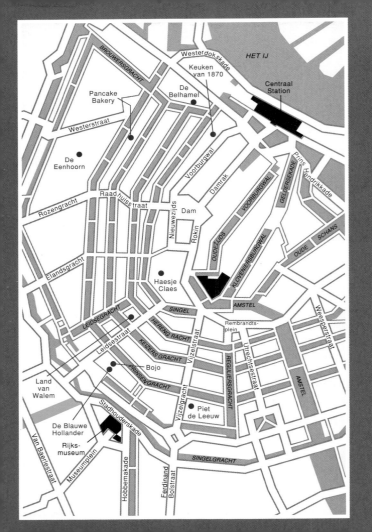

Inexpensive

KEUKEN VAN 1870 Spuistraat 4.
1130-2000 Mon.-Fri., 1600-2100 Sat. & Sun. Tram 1, 2, 5.
Simple Dutch food, basic surroundings, absolutely rock-bottom prices.

DE BLAUWE HOLLANDER Leidsekruisstraat 28.
1700-2200. Tram 1, 2, 5.
Generous portions of hearty Dutch stews are a speciality.

DE BELHAMEL Brouwersgracht 60.
1200-2400. Bus 18, 22.
Surprisingly good international cuisine at reasonable prices, served in a convivial atmosphere.

DE EENHOORN Tweede Egelantiersdwarsstraat 6.
1730-2300. Tram 13, 14, 17.
The terrace is a special attraction during the summer. Extensive menu.

PIET DE LEEUW Noorderstraat 11.
1200-2330 Mon.-Fri., 1700-2330 Sat. & Sun. Tram 16, 24, 25.
Steakhouse which is also famed for its beef casseroles.

LAND VAN WALEM Keizersgracht 449.
0900-0100 Sun.-Fri., 0900-0200 Sat. Tram 1, 2, 5.
Fashionable restaurant with a terrace overlooking the canal.

PANCAKE BAKERY Prinsengracht 191.
1200-2130. Tram 13, 14, 17.
Delicious pancakes with a wide selection of sweet and savoury fillings.

HAESJE CLAES Nieuwezijds Voorburgwal 320.
1100-2200 Mon.-Sat., 1700-2130 Sun. Tram 4, 9, 16, 24, 25.
Dutch and other Continental dishes. Exceptionally good value.

BOJO Lange Leidsedwarsstraat 51.
1700-0200 Sun.-Thu., 1700-0530 Fri. & Sat. Tram 1, 2, 5.
Inexpensive Indonesian cuisine. Great for hungry late-night revellers.

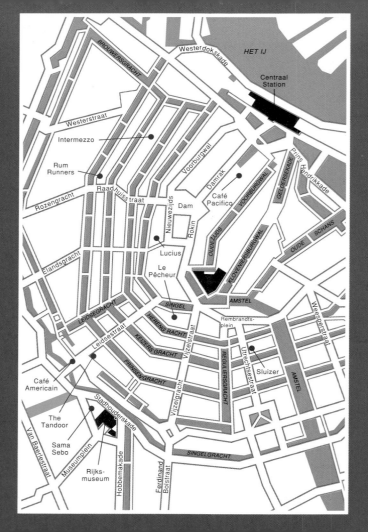

Moderate

CAFÉ AMERICAIN Leidsekade 97.
■ 1100-2400. Tram 1, 2, 5, 6, 7, 10.
International cuisine in the famous American Hotel (see MONUMENTS).

LE PÊCHEUR Reguliersdwarsstraat 32.
■ 1200-2300 Mon.-Fri., 1700-2400 Sat. & Sun. Tram 1, 2, 5.
Elegant seafood restaurant offering fresh, inventive dishes.

LUCIUS Spuistraat 247.
■ 1730-2300. Tram 13, 14, 17.
Fish and seafood specialities served in an attractive setting.

INTERMEZZO Herenstraat 28.
■ 1730-2200 Mon.-Fri., 1800-2230 Sat., 1800-2200 Sun. Tram 1, 2, 5.
French-Dutch cuisine and a refined atmosphere.

RUM RUNNERS Prinsengracht 277. ■ 1600-0100 Mon.-Thu.,
1200-2400 Fri. & Sat., 1200-0100 Sun. Tram 13, 14, 17.
A large, noisy eatery serving Caribbean dishes. Live music on Sun.

CAFÉ PACIFICO Warmoesstraat 31.
■ 1730-2300. Tram 4, 9, 16, 24, 25.
Probably the oldest, and one of the best Mexican restaurants in Europe.

THE TANDOOR Leidseplein 19.
■ 1730-2330. Tram 1, 2, 5.
Pleasant atmosphere. Good tandoori dishes and many other Asian specialities.

SAMA SEBO Hobbemastraat 10.
■ 1200-1400, 1800-2200 Mon.-Sat. Tram 1, 2, 5.
Famous Indonesian restaurant. Trendy setting and reasonable prices.

SLUIZER Utrechtsestraat 43-45.
■ 1100-2400 Mon.-Fri., 1700-2400 Sat. & Sun. Tram 4.
Two restaurants offering Dutch cuisine and seafood.

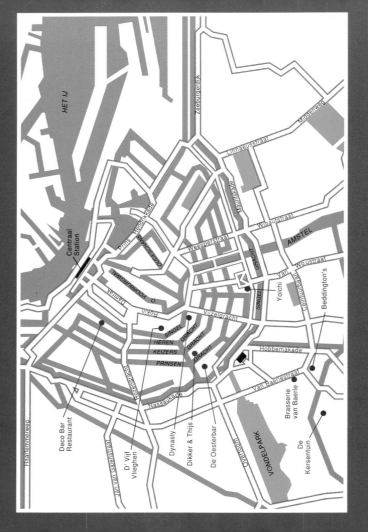

Expensive

BRASSERIE VAN BAERLE Van Baerlestraat 158.
■ 1200-2300 Mon.-Fri., 1000-2300 Sun. Tram 2, 3, 5.
Elegant décor, innovative cuisine, charming and attentive service.

D' VIJF VLIEGHEN Spuistraat 294 (enter by Vijf Vlieghensteeg).
■ 1800-2230. Tram 1, 2, 5.
Traditional Dutch dishes served in traditional Dutch surroundings.

YOICHI Weteringschans 128.
■ 1800-2400 Thu.-Sun. Tram 6, 7, 10.
One of the oldest and best Japanese restaurants in the city; book early.

DYNASTY Reguliersdwarsstraat 30.
■ 1300-2300 Wed.-Mon. Tram 1, 2, 5.
Cantonese haute cuisine. Sumptuous décor.

DE OESTERBAR Leidseplein 10.
■ 1200-2400. Tram 1, 2, 5, 7, 10.
*One of the very best seafood restaurants in town, overlooking the busy
Leidseplein (see **A-Z**).*

DE KERSENTUIN Dijsselhofplantsoen 7.
■ 1200-1430, 1800-2230 Mon.-Fri., 1800-2230 Sat. Tram 16; Bus 66.
Luxurious restaurant in five-star Garden Hotel. Serves nouvelle cuisine.

DECO BAR RESTAURANT Herengracht 117.
■ 1700-late Tue.-Sun. Tram 1, 2, 5, 13, 17.
Dine in style in Art Deco surroundings.

DIKKER & THIJS Prinsengracht 444.
■ 1800-2230 Mon.-Sat. Tram 1, 2, 5.
Old-fashioned attentive service and well-prepared Continental dishes.

BEDDINGTON'S Roelof Haartstraat 6.
■ 1200-1400, 1800-2200 Mon.-Sat. Tram 3, 12, 16, 24.
Sophisticated French and Asian specialities in a chic modern setting.

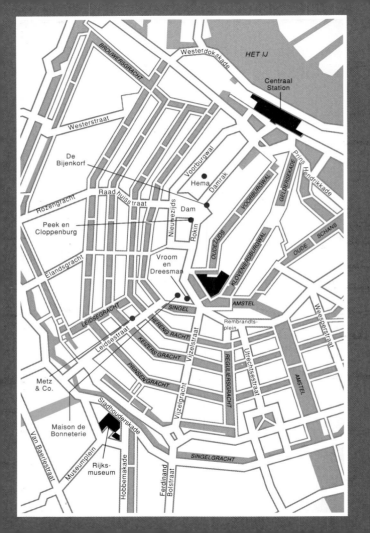

Department Stores

DE BIJENKORF Damrak 90.
■ 1100-1800 Mon., 0930-1800 Tue.-Fri. (2100 Thu.), 0900-1700 Sat.
Tram 4, 9, 16, 24, 25.
The biggest, and arguably the best, department store in Amsterdam.
Check out the regular snap sales, the high-class cafeteria and the bargain
'basement' in the attic. See **WALK 2**.

MAISON DE BONNETERIE Kalverstraat 183/Rokin 140-42.
▩ 1300-1730 Mon., 0930-1730 Tue.-Fri. (2100 Thu.), 0930-1700 Sat.
Tram 4, 9, 16, 24, 25.
Elegant and pricey store with a range of good-quality classical clothing.
Rather conservative.

METZ & CO. Keizersgracht 455.
■ 1100-1800 Mon., 0930-1800 Tue.-Fri. (2100 Thu.), 0930-1700 Sat.
Tram 1, 2, 5.
Ideal for gifts, prints and furnishings. The sixth-floor coffee shop has an
excellent view over the canals.

VROOM EN DREESMAN Kalverstraat 201.
■ 1100-1800 Mon., 0930-1800 Tue.-Fri. (2100 Thu.), 0900-1700 Sat.
Tram 4, 9, 16, 24, 25.
A large branch of a national chain of department stores. Clothes, books
and records at reasonable prices.

PEEK EN CLOPPENBURG Dam Square.
■ 1100-1800 Mon., 0930-1800 Tue.-Fri. (2100 Thu.), 0900-1700 Sat.
Tram 4, 9, 16, 24, 25.
Mainstream store good for middle-of-the-range clothing for all members
of the family.

HEMA Nieuwendijk 174-76.
■ 1100-1800 Mon., 0930-1800 Tue.-Fri. (2100 Thu.), 0900-1700 Sat.
Tram 4, 9, 16, 24, 25.
One of the biggest branches of this general-goods chain store which is
practically a national institution.

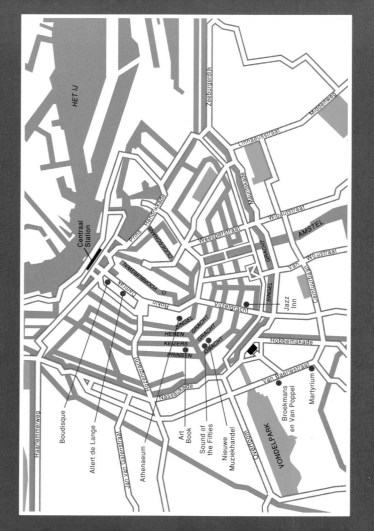

Books & Records

ART BOOK Prinsengracht 645.
▦ 1300-1800 Mon., 1100-1800 Tue.-Sat. Tram 16, 24, 25.
A wide selection of books on 20thC art.

ATHENAEUM Spui 14-16. ▦ 1300-1800 Mon., 0900-1800 Tue.-Fri.
(2100 Thu.), 0900-1700 Sat. Tram 1, 2, 5.
*General bookshop, with a newsagent selling international publications
next door (0800-2200 Mon.-Sat., 1000-1800 Sun.). See* **WALK 3.**

MARTYRIUM Van Baerlestraat 170.
▦ 0900-1800 Mon.-Fri., 0900-1700 Sat. Tram 3, 5, 12.
The best bookshop in this elegant part of town.

ALLERT DE LANGE Damrak 62.
▦ 1300-1800 Mon., 0900-1800 Tue.-Fri., 0900-1700 Sat. Tram 4, 9.
Excellent selection of maps and guides as well as books.

SOUND OF THE FIFTIES Prinsengracht 669.
▦ 0930-1800 Mon.-Fri. (2100 Thu.), 0930-1700 Sat. Tram 1, 2, 5.
New and second-hand records – Blues, jazz and rock 'n' roll.

BOUDISQUE Haringpakkerssteeg 10-18. ▦ 1300-1800 Mon., 1000-
1800 Tue.-Fri. (2100 Thu.), 1000-1700 Sat. Tram 4, 9, 16, 24, 25.
Caters for every taste in contemporary music. Good for unusual imports.

NIEUWE MUZIEKHANDEL Leidsestraat 50. ▦ 1300-1800 Mon.,
0900-1800 Tue.-Fri. (plus 1900-2100 Thu.), 0900-1700 Sat. Tram 1, 2, 5.
Classical records, tapes and compact discs. Also sells concert tickets.

BROEKMANS EN VAN POPPEL Van Baerlestraat 92-94.
▦ 1000-1800 Mon., 0900-1800 Tue.-Fri., 0900-1700 Sat. Tram 3, 5.
Deals only in classical CDs.

JAZZ INN Vijzelgracht 9. ▦ 1230-1800 Mon., 1100-1800 Tue.-Fri.
(2100 Thu.), 1000-1700 Sat. Tram 16, 24.
Traditional and contemporary jazz.

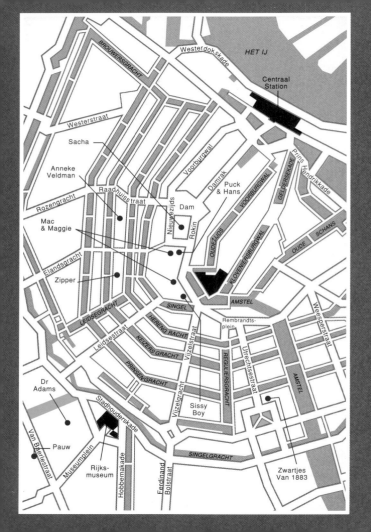

Clothes

MAC & MAGGIE Kalverstraat 53 & 172. ■ 1300-1700 Mon., 0900-1800 Tue.-Fri., 0900-1700 Sat. Tram 4, 9, 14.
Branches of a nationwide chain selling moderately-priced casual wear.

SISSY BOY Kalverstraat 210. ■ 1300-1800 Mon., 0900-1800 Tue.-Fri., 0900-1700 Sat. Tram 4, 9, 14.
Sport and leisure clothing.

SACHA Kalverstraat 20 & 161. ■ 1300-1800 Mon., 0900-1800 Tue.-Fri., 0900-1700 Sat. Tram 4, 9, 14.
Youthful, stylish footwear at reasonable prices.

DR ADAMS Pieter Cornelisz Hooftstraat 90. ■ 1300-1800 Mon., 0900-1800 Tue.-Fri. (2100 Thu.), 0900-1700 Sat. Tram 2, 3, 5.
Up-market modern and designer shoes.

PAUW Van Baerlestraat 48, 66, 72 & 90.
■ 1300-1800 Mon., 0900-1800 Tue.-Fri., 0900-1700 Sat. Tram 2, 3, 5.
Fairly exclusive selection of designer clothing. The branch at No. 48 has children's clothes.

ZWARTJES VAN 1883 Utrechtsestraat 123. ■ 1300-1800 Mon., 0900-1800 Tue.-Fri. (2100 Thu.), 0900-1700 Sat. Tram 4.
Quality footwear. Also has a good children's department.

ANNEKE VELDMAN Hartenstraat 30.
■ 1100-1800 Mon.-Fri., 1100-1700 Sat. Tram 13, 14, 17.
Original designs and leather clothing.

PUCK & HANS Rokin 66. ■ 1300-1800 Mon., 1030-1800 Tue.-Fri., 1000-1700 Sat. Tram 4, 9, 14.
Well-established in fashion circles. Has Parisian and own designer labels.

ZIPPER Huidenstraat 7.
■ 1300-1800 Mon., 0930-1800 Tue.-Fri., 1100-1800 Sat. Tram 1, 2, 5.
Specialist in second-hand American classics.

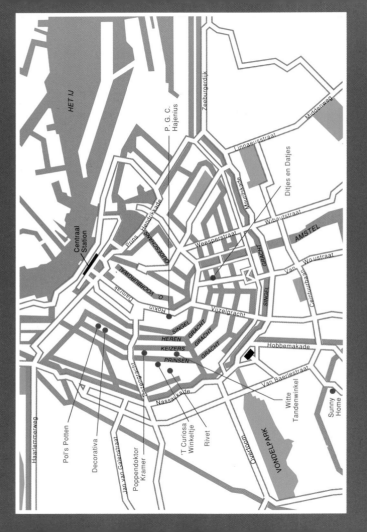

Gifts

RIVET Elandsgracht 69.
■ 1200-1700 Wed.-Sat. (1400-1700 Thu.). Tram 10, 17.
Leather goods – some imported, some designed in-house.

P. G. C. HAJENIUS Rokin 94-96.
■ 0900-1800 Mon.-Fri., 0900-1700 Sat. Tram 4, 9, 14, 16, 24, 25.
*Tobacco and smokers' accessories. (The Netherlands is famous for its cigars and tobacco – see **Best Buys**.)*

WITTE TANDENWINKEL Runstraat 5.
■ 1300-1800 Mon., 1000-1800 Tue.-Sat. Tram 1, 2, 5.
Everything for healthy teeth, including jokey items like whisky toothpaste.

DECORATIVA Herenstraat 27.
■ 0830-1800. Tram 1, 2, 5, 13, 17.
One of the prettiest window displays in town. Sells flowers and antiques.

POL'S POTTEN Herenstraat 30.
■ 1030-1800 Mon.-Fri., 1030-1700 Sat. Tram 1, 2, 5, 13, 17.
Pots, jars and other terracotta items.

'T CURIOSA WINKELTJE Prinsengracht 228.
■ 1000-1730 Tue.-Fri., 1000-1700 Sat. Tram 13, 14, 17.
Charmingly cramped gift shop with a delightful selection of curiosities.

DITJES EN DATJES Utrechtsestraat 53.
■ 1100-1800 Tue.-Fri., 1100-1700 Sat. Tram 4.
Household gifts and bric-a-brac.

SUNNY HOME Beethovenstraat 10.
■ 0900-1800 Tue.-Fri., 1000-1700 Sat. Tram 5.
Modern and designer goods for the home.

POPPENDOKTOR KRAMER Reestraat 20.
■ 1000-1800 Tue.-Fri., 1000-1700 Sat. Tram 13, 14, 17.
Huge collection of toys, dolls and puppets, some of them antique.

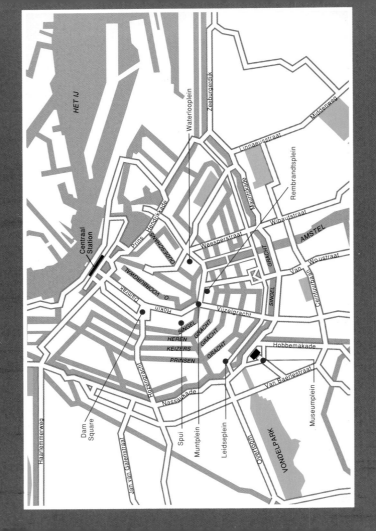

DAM SQUARE

Tram 1, 2, 4, 5, 9, 16, 24, 25.
The bustling heart of the city, overlooked by the Koninklijk Paleis (see **A-Z***) and Nieuwe Kerk (see* CHURCHES*). Often crammed with all kinds of street entertainers. See* WALK 2*,* **A-Z***.*

LEIDSEPLEIN

Tram 1, 2, 5, 7, 10.
One of the city's major nightlife centres – teeming with cinemas, theatres, restaurants and clubs. See **A-Z***.*

REMBRANDTSPLEIN

Tram 4, 9, 14.
The statue of the great artist (see **Rembrandt***) is surrounded by cafés, restaurants and 'topless' bars. See* WALK 5*,* **A-Z***.*

MUNTPLEIN

Tram 4, 9, 14, 16, 24, 25.
Beside the Drijvende Bloemenmarkt (see **A-Z***) and straddling the waterways, this is the site of the Munttoren (see* **A-Z***).*

SPUI

Tram 1, 2, 5.
Café Hoppe (see CAFÉS*) and the Begijnhof (see* **A-Z***) are two of this busy junction's main attractions. Relax in one of them and watch the world go by. See* WALK 3*.*

WATERLOOPLEIN

Tram 9, 14; M Waterlooplein.
The heart of the Jewish Quarter (see CITY DISTRICTS*) and home of the Flea Market (see* **A-Z***).*

MUSEUMPLEIN

Tram 3, 5, 12.
Major museums (see MUSEUMS 1*) are surrounded by the exclusive shopping streets of P. C. Hooftstraat, Beethovenstraat and Van Baerlestraat.*

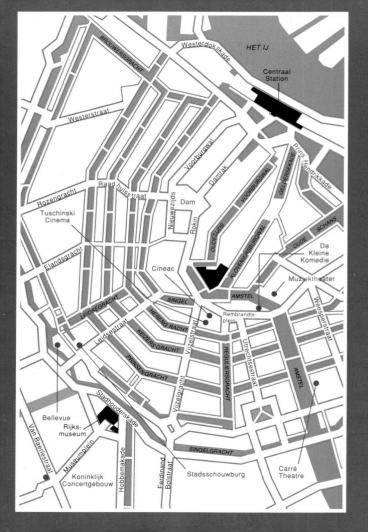

KONINKLIJK CONCERTGEBOUW Van Baerlestraat 98.
Tram 3, 5, 12, 16. ● f15-f50.
*Internationally renowned concert hall with superb acoustics. Sometimes
features rock as well as classical music. See* **OFFICIAL BUILDINGS**, **A-Z**.

MUZIEKTHEATER Waterlooplein.
Tram 9, 14; **M** Waterlooplein. ● f20-f50.
*New opera house (opened 1986) offering the best in theatre and dance.
See* **OFFICIAL BUILDINGS**.

CARRÉ THEATRE Amstel 115-25.
Tram 4; **M** Weesperplein. ● f20-f50.
*Amsterdam's answer to Broadway – this theatre specializes in presenting
major popular musicals.*

STADSSCHOUWBURG Leidseplein 26.
Tram 1, 2, 5. ● f10-f30.
*A classical playhouse offering a wide selection of theatre, dance and
musical events.*

BELLEVUE Leidsekade 90.
Tram 1, 2, 5. ● f15-f20.
Sometimes stages English-language theatre productions.

DE KLEINE KOMEDIE Amstel 56.
Tram 4, 9, 14, 16, 24, 25. ● f15-f20.
Satirical revues and comedies, often performed in English.

TUSCHINSKI CINEMA Reguliersbreestraat 26.
Tram 4, 9, 14, 16, 24, 25. ● f5-f15.
*Six screens mostly showing international mainstream films in a building
which is itself a work of art. See* **MONUMENTS**, **WALK 5**.

CINEAC Reguliersbreestraat 31.
Tram 4, 9, 14, 16, 24, 25. ● f5-f15.
Has the same owners as the nearby Tuschinski cinema (see above).

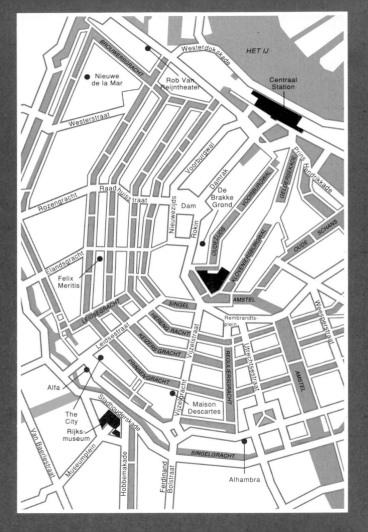

THEATRE & CINEMA 2

THE CITY Kleine Gartmanplantsoen 13-25.
Tram 1, 2, 5, 6, 7, 10. ● f5-f15.
Multiscreen complex in an Art Deco building.

ALFA Hirschgebouw, Kleine Gartmanplantsoen.
Tram 1, 2, 5, 6, 7, 10. ● f5-f15.
Shows a variety of mainstream international films.

ALHAMBRA Weteringschans 134.
Tram 4. ● f5-f15.
Two screens and a constantly changing programme.

FELIX MERITIS Keizersgracht 324.
Tram 1, 2, 5. ● f10-f15.
Four auditoriums where anything can happen: from mime to drama, to dance, to circuses. The venue is also the organizer of and base for the Amsterdam summer university. See **WALK 5.**

NIEUWE DE LA MAR Marnixstraat 404.
Tram 1, 2, 5.
Cabaret, music and occasional English-language productions.

MAISON DESCARTES Vijzelgracht 2a.
Tram 16, 24, 25. ● f10-f20.
Film shows and theatrical performances organized by the French consulate to promote French culture and Dutch classics.

DE BRAKKE GROND Nes 45.
Tram 4, 9, 16, 24, 25.
Centre for the promotion of Flemish culture which often has theatrical presentations.

ROB VAN REIJNTHEATER Haarlemerdijk 31.
Tram 3; Bus 18, 22, 44.
Originally a pantomime showcase, this theatre now presents a wider range of shows, including frequent English-language productions.

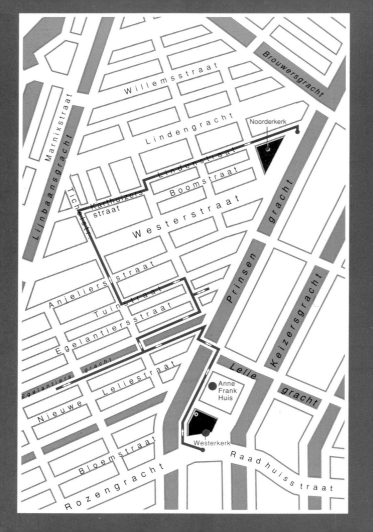

The Jordaan

Duration: Approximately 2 hr.

Start at the Westerkerk (see **CHURCHES**), which is worth visiting not least for the view from the top of its impressive tower. Rembrandt (see **A-Z**) is supposed to be buried here, but the only evidence of this is a memorial plaque. The Homomonument (see **MONUMENTS**) stands outside on the Westermarkt.

The Westerkerk is situated beside the outermost of Amsterdam's girdle of main canals, the Prinsengracht (see **CANALS & RIVERS**), which forms the eastern boundary of the popular and lively district of the Jordaan (see **A-Z**). Before entering this part of town, turn right and walk along the canal until you come to Anne Frank Huis (see **MUSEUMS 1**). There is often a queue of sightseers waiting to get into this small museum, a 'must' for most visitors to Amsterdam.

Cross the canal by the nearest bridge, turn right and then immediately left, and you are on Egelantiersgracht, a smaller canal taking you into the Jordaan. The narrow streets and attractive houses make this a very pleasant area for a stroll, and there are numerous cafés and small shops to enjoy.

The more interesting buildings on Egelantiersgracht are on the odd-numbered side of the street. The façades of the 'Three Houses' at Nos 61-65 are embellished with wild animals. The former Beguine convent of St. Andrieshofje, which has an accessible courtyard, stands further along at No. 107. Retrace your steps and cross the canal by the Hilletjes Bridge before continuing along the even-numbered side to Eerste Egelantiersdwarsstraat on your left. Standing on the corner is the Café 'T Smalle, a distillery founded in 1780 which is famous for its juniper liqueur.

Turn right along Egelantiersstraat, the first street you come to, and stop to admire the 17thC gable at No. 52, which depicts a hand writing a letter. Next door is the entrance to the Claes Claershofje (or Ansloshofje), founded in 1626 and the second Beguine convent of the tour. It was originally the residence of Claes Claersz Anslo, a cloth merchant. Nowadays it provides accommodation for art students. Inside the courtyard there is another exit to the left which takes you back onto Eerste Egelantiersdwarsstraat. Turn right and you soon come to Tuinstraat. Turn left to reach another Beguine convent, the

Westerkerk

Regenboogsliefdehofje at Nos 100-02. It is closed to the public, but some bolder visitors do wander inside for a look around.

Next, turn right at Tweede Tuindwarsstraat and go straight ahead across the Westerstraat to Tichelstraat. There are some interesting gables and façades at Nos 53 and 33. Turn right into Karthuizersstraat and you will see the Huiszittenweduwenhof (Courtyard of Widows) on your right. It was built in 1650 and is well preserved.

Continue along Karthuizersstraat and Lindenstraat until you reach the Noorderkerk (see **CHURCHES**), Noordermarkt and Prinsengracht.

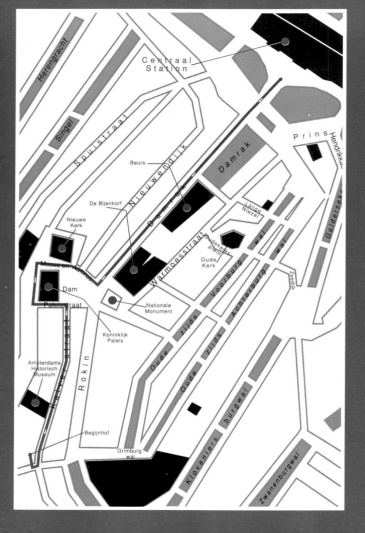

The Heart of the City

Duration: Approximately 1 hr.

Opposite Centraal station (see **OFFICIAL BUILDINGS**) you will see Damrak, the main thoroughfare leading to Dam Square (see **A-Z**). Follow it, and on the way take a look at the façade of the office building on the right at Nos 28-25 – you will see four baboons and 22 owls staring down at you! Opposite is the stock exchange building, Beurs (see **OFFICIAL BUILDINGS**), which dates from 1903. It still looks modern so it is easy to see why it originally aroused such controversy. In front is the Beursplein, which is a favourite with roller skaters, and at the other end of the square, De Bijenkorf (see **SHOPPING 1**). On the pavement opposite stands the statue of a man with a newspaper under his arm, which was donated to the city by the newspaper *Financiaal Dagblad*.

Continue along the Damrak until you reach Dam Square. To your left is the Nationale Monument (see **MONUMENTS**), inside of which are enclosed 12 urns of soil, one from each of the country's provinces and one from the former colony of Indonesia. Facing the monument is the Koninklijk Paleis (see **A-Z**) and next to it the Nieuwe Kerk (see **CHURCHES**). On either side of the church at Gravenstraat 125 are what appear to be Amsterdam's smallest shops. Take the Mozes en Aäronstraat between the church and the palace and you come out on Nieuwezijds Voorburgwal in front of what used to be the Main Post Office (see **OFFICIAL BUILDINGS**), with its pear-shaped towers. The curious Spaarpottenmuseum (see **MUSEUMS 4**) stands on the other side of Raadhuisstraat. Don't cross the street, but instead turn left round the back of the palace and return to Dam Square via Paleisstraat.

The first street on the right is Kalverstraat, a pedestrian precinct crammed with a variety of shops. Look out for the porch at No. 92. It dates from 1592 and is the entrance to a former orphanage which is now the Amsterdams Historisch Museum (see **MUSEUMS 2**). Continue along Kalverstraat, turn right at the first main intersection and you are on Spui (see **SQUARES**). Scan the wall on your right for the small door at No. 14 which is the entrance to the Begijnhof (see **A-Z**). Explore the Engelse Kerk (see **CHURCHES**) and the Catholic church before taking a look at the oldest house in the city at No. 34 – its wooden gable dates from about 1475.

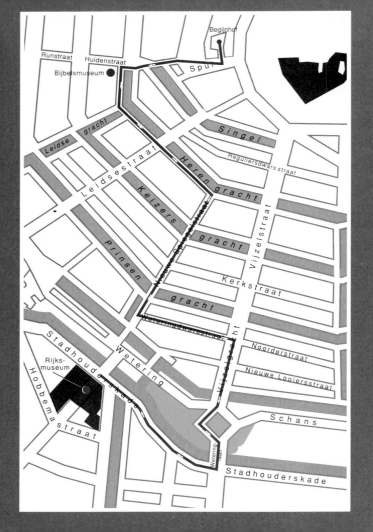

Spui to Museumplein

Duration: Approximately 1 hr.
Begin your walk with a visit to the Begijnhof (see **A-Z**) off Spui (see **SQUARES**), before going into the square for a look at Het Lieverdje – Amsterdam's 'Little Darling' (see **MONUMENTS**). Head for Café Hoppe (see **CAFÉS**), passing the Athenaeum bookshop (see **SHOPPING 2**) on your right. Cross Spuistraat and take Heisteeg, a narrow passage, over the Singel (see **CANALS & RIVERS**). Carry straight on to Wijde Heisteeg. No. 4 has a sign outside depicting a yawning man and used to be an apothecary's shop. When you reach the bridge over the Herengracht (see **CANALS & RIVERS**) stop to admire the view of the canal and the various types of gable (see **A-Z**) on the houses lining it. Turn left after the bridge and look out for the Bijbelsmuseum (see **MUSEUMS 2**), to be found at No. 366.
No. 380, built in the 19thC for a rich tobacco planter, is decorated with sculptures of double-headed angels. Nos 390-2 have neck gables depicting a man and a woman in 17thC costume. Continue along the Herengracht past the Leidsegracht and Leidsestraat until you come to the famous Golden Bend, where the most expensive and magnificent houses in Amsterdam were built in the 17thC. Note the double stairways and the splendid entrances.
Next turn right and follow the Nieuwe Spiegelstraat, which contains many antique shops. The Rijksmuseum (see **A-Z**) is ahead of you at the far end of the street. Walk towards it, passing Kerkstraat (which is beginning to rival Nieuwe Spiegelstraat for antique dealers) and turn left into Eerste Weteringdwarsstraat where there is an old secret Beguine convent at Nos. 19-35. Push open the gate of the Grilshofje (as it is called) and enter through the porch, respecting the quiet of the courtyard. Notice the unique Louis XVI clock.
Back on Eerste Weteringdwarsstraat continue on to Vijzelgracht which runs south from Muntplein (see **SQUARES**) to the Singelgracht (not to be confused with the Singel).
Turn right into Vijzelgracht, walk to the bridge, and the Rijksmuseum is the immense building on your right. Beyond it is the Museumplein district (see **CITY DISTRICTS**), where you will find the renowned Van Gogh and Stedelijk museums (see **A-Z**), and the equally famous Koninklijk Concertgebouw (see **A-Z**).

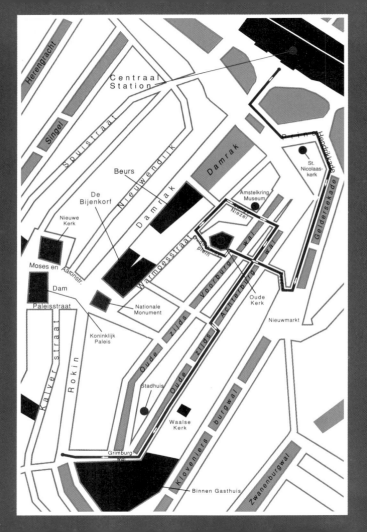

The Red-light District

Duration: Approximately 1 hr 30 min.

From Centraal station (see **OFFICIAL BUILDINGS**) turn left along Prins Hendrikkade towards the Oosterdok and you will see the St. Nicolaaskerk (see **CHURCHES**). A little further on, at the head of the Geldersekade, is the Schreierstoren (see **A-Z**), the unofficial entrance to Amsterdam's notorious Red-light District (see **A-Z**). Walk along the right-hand side of the Geldersekade until you reach Nieuwmarkt (see **Markets**). Drug pushers are a common sight here, so you may not wish to linger too long. Turn sharp right along the Zeedijk for a few metres, and then go left along Molensteeg. This takes you across the canals to the imposing Oude Kerk (see **CHURCHES**), Amsterdam's oldest and largest church.

The tiny Wijde Kerksteg behind the church leads to Warmoesstraat, which was once the most desirable address in the city, but is now decidedly seedy. There is an attractive tea and coffee shop at No. 66. The façade of the house opposite, which was once the residence of a cloth merchant, is embellished with a carved ox head. Go north along Warmoesstraat in the direction of Centraal station and take the second turning on the right into Lange Niezel. The Amstelkring Museum (see **MUSEUMS 2**) stands on the left where the street rejoins Oudezijds Voorburgwal. Known as 'Our Dear Lord in the Attic', this is one of the most interesting of Amsterdam's small museums.

Cross the canal, head along Korte Niezel, and turn right along the Oudezijds Achterburgwal into the centre of the red-light area, where prostitutes sit impassively in the windows advertising their availability. Two 17thC warehouses stand near the junction with Molensteeg. One of them has a bas-relief of a boat caught in a storm, and a fortress with the inscription 'God is my Castle'. Next to it is the 'Old Sailor', containing maritime souvenirs (there is a model ship above the entrance).

Cross the canal and head south, passing the Waalse Kerk on your left and the Stadhuis (see **OFFICIAL BUILDINGS**) on your right, until you reach the Grimburgwal. To the left is the former Binnen Gasthuis hospital, now university buildings. Cross the bridge towards Oudezijds Voorburgwal again and you will see the 'House of Three Canals'. Ahead is Langebrugsteeg, which leads to the busy thoroughfare of Rokin.

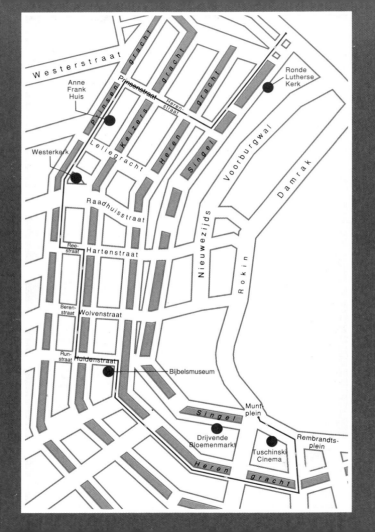

The Main Canals

Duration: Approximately 4 hr.

Start at the northern end of the Singel (see **CANALS & RIVERS**), where you will see the Ronde Lutherse Kerk (see **CHURCHES**) on your left. The best view is from the other side of the canal. Very near the church, at Singel 7, there is a remarkably narrow house which is a popular subject for holiday snaps. Continue south along the canal as far as Blauwburgwal and then turn right, crossing the Herengracht (see **CANALS & RIVERS**) and Keizersgracht (see **CANALS & RIVERS**) to reach the Prinsengracht (see **CANALS & RIVERS**). Turn left along the canal and stop to admire the 18thC courtyard at No. 159. Anne Frank Huis (see **MUSEUMS 1**) and the Westerkerk (see **CHURCHES**) are further along on the same side of the street. After the busy Raadhuisstraat, turn left at Reestraat to reach Keizersgracht once more. Turn right and enjoy the views of the fine buildings on both sides of the canal – especially of Felix Meritis (see **THEATRE & CINEMA 2**). The side streets along here contain interesting little shops (see **SHOPPING 4**). Take Huidenstraat on the left to reach Herengracht at the point where the famous Golden Bend, with its superb 17thC houses, begins. The Bijbelsmuseum (see **MUSEUMS 2**) is on your right, and the stretch of canal from here to Vijzelstraat is lined with many opulent mansions. Next on the right after Vijzelgracht is the Reguliersgracht (see **CANALS & RIVERS**), with its famous view of seven canal bridges in a row. Head in the opposite direction, along the garish Thorbeckeplein, and turn left after Rembrandtsplein (see **A-Z**) into Reguliersbreestraat, home of the famous Tuschinski Cinema (see **MONUMENTS**). This street leads to Muntplein (see **SQUARES**) at the southern end of the Singel. The Drijvende Bloemenmarkt (see **A-Z**) on the left bank creates a bustling, colourful scene.

Aalsmeer: 16 km southwest of Amsterdam. Pop: 21,000. A town near Schiphol (see **Airport**) notable for the Bloemenveiling (flower auction) held all year round in the enormous auction hall at Legmeerdijk 313 (0730-1100 Mon.-Fri.). A visitors' gallery gives a splendid view of the trading area, with its spectacular and colourful arrays of flowers. See EXCURSION 3.

Alkmaar: 35 km north of Amsterdam. Pop: 84,000. A well-preserved town, established by the 13thC, with much to interest the visitor.
The St. Laurenskerk (1470-1516), also called the Grote Kerk, is Gothic in style, and includes a 17thC organ and pulpit, and a vault painting by Cornelis Buys.
The Stedelijk Museum at Doelenstraat 3 has exhibits on town history and paintings by many of the lesser lights of the Golden Age. The tower of the Waag (public weighing-house) in the main square features clockwork jousting knights. A great attraction is the Kaasmarkt (cheese market), held in the Waagplein every Fri. morning during the summer months.
The pleasant coastal resorts of Egmond aan Zee and Bergen aan Zee are to be found just outside Alkmaar. See EXCURSION 2.

Alphen aan de Rijn: 36 km southwest of Amsterdam. Pop: 55,000. The main attraction of this town is the Avifauna bird sanctuary, which contains nearly 300 species of birds, many of them exotic, and keeps them in conditions sympathetic to their accustomed habitats in the wild. It is open all year round, until 2100 during the summer months and 1800 in winter.

Amersfoort: 41 km southeast of Amsterdam. Pop: 87,000. A pleasant town with many canals, squares and quaint little streets. The St. Joriskerk dates mainly from the 15th and 16thC, but the tower has stonework from the mid-13thC. The Koppelpoort, an ancient water gate over the river Eem, was restored in the late 19thC by P. J. H. Cuypers (see **Architecture**). Historic and prehistoric artefacts from Amersfoort and the nearby city of Utrecht (see **A-Z**) can be seen in the Museum Flehite at Westsingel 50.

Architecture: Although Amsterdam's Gothic remains suggest that the buildings of earlier times were impressive, it was the architecture of Hendrick de Keyser, Jacob van Campen and Philips Vingboons, who were responsible for introducing the Renaissance styles in the 17thC, which really established the city as a centre of excellence in this field. Examples of their work include the Munttoren (see **A-Z**), the Koninklijk Paleis (see **A-Z**) and the Westerkerk, Noorderkerk and Zuiderkerk (see **CHURCHES**).

The next great advance was the neo-Gothic style of P. J. H. Cuypers in the late 19thC, which was superseded by the highly influential Hendrik P. Berlage, who ushered in a new era of architecture with his innovative design for the Beurs (see **OFFICIAL BUILDINGS**).

A group inspired by Berlage, and known as the Amsterdam School, produced some outstanding housing developments in a frantic burst of creativity around the 1920s. To the fore of the group were Michael de Klerk and P. L. Kramer (see **CITY DISTRICTS**).

Succeeding movements, such as the group known as De Stijl, reacted

against the elaborate style of the Amsterdam School. Their more functional approach to design is echoed in Gerrit Rietveld's Van Gogh Museum (see **A-Z**).
Development continues today, and there is much to admire in the blending of new buildings with the old in many parts of Amsterdam, such as the Jordaan (see **A-Z**).

Begijnhof: Situated off Spui (see SQUARES), the Begijnhof is a quiet courtyard in a former convent for Beguine nuns. A secret chapel (see **Religious Services**) was built following the Reformation, and the main church, the Engelse Kerk (see CHURCHES, **Religious Services**), was taken over by Scottish Presbyterians. Both can be visited, as can one of Amsterdam's oldest houses – a wooden structure originally built in the late 15thC. However, the main attraction of the Begijnhof may well be the peace and quiet of this secluded area lying right in the heart of the city. See MONUMENTS, WALKS 2 & 3.

Bicycles: An ideal way to see Amsterdam, because of the compact nature of the city and the excellent facilities provided for cyclists. A charming feature of the city is the sight of swarms of Amsterdammers fearlessly weaving in and out of the busy traffic. Inexperienced riders will find that the many cycle lanes make life easier. The entire country is geared to the bicycle, and all the trains will accommodate them if you want to go further afield. You must have reflectors on your wheels and keep in single file at all times (even in cycle lanes). See **Bicycle Hire**.

Brown Cafés: So called because of their dark wooden furnishings and nicotine-stained walls. Many of these traditional cafés are centuries old. Although sparsely decorated, they provide a friendly and relaxed atmosphere, and are ideal places for a coffee or a quiet drink during the day, or a chat with locals during the evening. Most provide basic snacks, if not full meals. You will find a brown café on virtually every corner in the Jordaan (see **A-Z**), although some of these tend to be rather artificial versions of the real thing, which is typified by the famous Café Hoppe (see CAFÉS).

Canals: Amsterdam abounds in waterways, but the only natural one is the Amstel river. The town began to grow after this was dammed in the 13thC, and a ring of canals (*grachtengordel*) was built as the city expanded. From the centre outwards, these are the Singel, Herengracht, Keizersgracht and Prinsengracht. They are lined with fine merchants' houses and large warehouses, providing many attractive views. The Brouwersgracht, which runs along the north end of the main canals, and other minor canals running through the Red-light District (see **A-Z**), the old town and the dockland areas east of the city centre, are especially picturesque. Nowadays there is little commercial traffic on the canals, but you will often see boatloads of sightseers passing along them. For many people this is one of the most fascinating ways to see the city (and places of interest along the way are pointed out by the guides). See **CANALS & RIVERS**, **CHILDREN**, **Canal Bike Hire**, **Tours & Excursions**.

Dam Square: Known by the locals simply as Dam. It was on this site that the Amstel river (see **CANALS & RIVERS**) was dammed in the 13thC, starting the growth of the city (see **History**). The Stadhuis, or town hall, was built on the square and later converted to the Koninklijk Paleis (see **A-Z**). Next door is the Nieuwe Kerk (see **CHURCHES**), which serves as the royal chapel and is the location for State occasions such as the 1980 coronation of Queen Beatrix. Opposite is the Nationale Monument (see **MONUMENTS**). Dam is the real heart of the city, and a good starting point for visiting the main shopping streets, the main canals and the old town (see CITY DISTRICTS). Many trams (see A-Z) pass through the square, which is often vibrant with street entertainment. See SQUARES, WALK 2.

Delft: 60 km southwest of Amsterdam. Pop: 86,000. This town near The Hague (see A-Z) has many attractions, not least of which is the famous pottery which bears its name (see **Best Buys**). Two Gothic churches, the Nieuwe Kerk and Oude Kerk, stand near each other in the town centre; and the main museums are the Prinsenhof and the Huis Lambert van Meerten. The former is notable as the place where William the Silent, Prince of Orange, was assassinated in 1584. Historical artefacts are exhibited here. The Huis Lambert van Meerten has impressive displays of Delftware. The pottery can also be admired (and bought) at numerous factory showrooms and shops (see **Best Buys**). The prettiness of Delft makes it a pleasant place for a leisurely stroll. Some of its street scenes were painted by Vermeer (see A-Z), the town's most famous son, and the atmosphere he captured has certainly survived.

Diamonds: Amsterdam has been associated with diamonds since the 16thC, when Jewish immigrants first introduced the trade to the city. The discovery of diamonds in South Africa in the 1860s heralded a time of expansion for the industry, with Amsterdam very much to the fore. The biggest diamond ever discovered, the Cullinan, was cut here (as was the famous Kohinoor) and the city remains one of the world's foremost centres for this glamorous trade. Guided tours of the factories enable you to admire the skills of the craftsmen as they cut and polish the precious stones. There are also numerous diamond shops in the city centre should you wish to buy or just window-shop. See **Best Buys**.

Drijvende Bloemenmarkt (Floating Flower Market):
Located on the Singel (see CANALS & RIVERS) between Muntplein (see SQUARES) and Koningsplein, and open 0900-1600 Mon.-Sat. A vast range of inexpensive bulbs, cuttings, flowers and pot plants is sold from stalls floating on the canal, making the market one of the city's most colourful sights. See WALK 5, **Best Buys**.

Dykes: Without its vast programme of land reclamation, the Netherlands as we know it would not exist. About half of its 13 million inhabitants live on land won back from the sea by means of the extensive system of dykes. Basically, the process involves walling off an area and draining it with pumps. The water is removed to the canals, which carry it eventually to the sea, and selected crops of reeds and rapeseed are sown to assist in the drying and reconditioning of the soil. The apparent simplicity of this system belies the reality of the continual struggle to keep the sea at bay. Pumping stations must operate constantly to prevent flooding, and freak weather conditions can have disastrous effects. For the visitor, the dyked Dutch countryside provides an opportunity for enjoying a vast flat landscape, often bathed in colour at flower-gathering time, which is ideal for the cyclist. Surprisingly large vessels make their way along the canals above the level of the road – impressive proof of the engineering achievements of the dyke builders.

Edam: 22 km northeast of Amsterdam. Pop: 24,000. This exceptionally pretty coastal town close to Volendam (see **A-Z**) on the Markermeer (see **A-Z**) is famous for giving its name to the round cheese, which is actually not as popular in the Netherlands as Gouda. The Kaasmarkt (cheese market) is one of its main attractions, as is the local museum at Damplein 8. Explore the town's canals and streets, which are lined with picturesque houses. See **EXCURSION 1**.

Enkhuizen: 62 km northeast of Amsterdam. Pop: 16,000. A harbour town on the IJsselmeer (see **A-Z**) whose main attraction is the remarkable Zuider Zee Museum, consisting of the Binnenmuseum (indoor) and the Buitenmuseum (outdoor). The former is housed in large converted warehouses surrounding a central courtyard, and exhibits maritime artefacts and furniture relating to the history of the area (1000-1700 Mon.-Sat., 1200-1700 Sun., April-Oct.). The Buitenmuseum can only be reached by ferry from the town's main jetty (1000-1700 April-Oct.). Here you can wander around reconstructions of local fishing villages. Shops sell traditional handicrafts as well as mass-produced souvenirs, and there are interesting demonstrations of crafts such as boat building. See **EXCURSION 1**.

Flea Market: Located on Waterlooplein (see **SQUARES**) alongside the Stadhuis/Muziektheater (see **OFFICIAL BUILDINGS**). Bargains are to be found among the stalls selling second-hand clothes, books, antiques and household goods, but haggling is not the done thing (1000-1600 Mon.-Sat.).

Food: Traditional Dutch food is fairly plain and filling, and you will not go hungry even on a restricted budget. Breakfast consists of eggs, cheese, various cold meats, and bread rolls and jam. Many kinds of snacks are sold on the streets, the speciality being seafood like herring (see **Maatjes**), mackerel and eel. A wide variety of *broodjes* (filled bread rolls) is also available. An *uitsmijter,* consisting of bread, fried eggs and a topping of ham or cheese, makes for an inexpensive meal. The most favoured cheeses are Edam and Gouda. Other staple dishes include thick soups, cold meats, sausages and waffles. A traditional dinner consists of typical northwestern European fare such as stews or grills; while a wide variety of ethnic restaurants provide a selection of more exotic dishes. See **RESTAURANTS 1-3**, **Eating Out**.

Frank, Anne (1929-45): Born into a Jewish family in Frankfurt, Anne Frank and her relations fled from the Nazis in 1933 and settled in Amsterdam. The Nazi occupation spelt further danger, and in 1942 the family took refuge in a secret back room at Prinsengracht 263 (see **MUSEUMS 1**) where Anne wrote her famous diary, which has become such an important testimony to the suffering of the Jews. The little group were betrayed to the Germans in 1944 and Anne died in Belsen concentration camp the following year. The house has been preserved just as it was in her time, and is undeniably a most moving place to visit. Exhibitions record the unfortunate continuation of racist and anti-Semitic thought in many quarters today.

Gables: Because canal houses were at one time taxed according to the widths of their façades, many of even the grandest houses were very narrow in construction. For a rich merchant, one way of compensating for this lack of frontage was to adorn the roof with an impressive gable to advertise his status. A walk along the canals will reveal the astonishing variety of shapes and styles employed: neck, column, bell, step and spout, to name but a few. Sculpted figures often illustrate the trade of the original occupant. See **Houses**.

Gouda: 50 km south of Amsterdam. Pop: 60,000. World-famous for its cheese, which the Dutch prefer to Edam. The cheese market is held in the market square every Thu. from June to Aug. (0900-1200). The nearby Gothic Stadhuis is supposed to be the oldest town hall in the Netherlands, and St. Janskerk boasts an impressive array of stained-glass windows, many predating the fire of 1552 which destroyed much of the church. The windows commissioned to replace those lost depict many of the outstanding figures of the mid-16thC.

Haarlem: 20 km west of Amsterdam. Pop: 152,000. Two of the major influences forming Haarlem's distinctive character are the tulip trade (see **A-Z**) and its nearby beach resort (see **Zandvoort**). The painter Franz Hals, who spent the greater part of his life here, has a museum named after him (converted from a hospice designed by another notable Haarlemmer, the architect Lieven de Key), which is dedicated to his life and work. The Teylers Museum at Spaarne 16 was founded in 1778, making it the oldest existing museum in the Netherlands. Unfortunately its antiquity is all too apparent, although it does contain some interesting exhibits of scientific instruments and some sketches by Rembrandt (see **A-Z**), Raphael and Michelangelo. Elsewhere, the Grote Kerk and its environs are evocative of the old Holland. Haarlem has the reputation of being a lively nightspot (especially enjoyable after a day on the beach at nearby Zandvoort), and is conveniently located for a trip south to the heart of the tulip country. See **EXCURSION 2**.

Hague, The: 60 km southwest of Amsterdam. Pop: 445,000. Known by the Dutch as Den Haag, rather than by its more formal name of 's-Gravenhage, this is an elegant city, as befits a seat of government and a centre of royal and State occasions. The parliament buildings, parts of which have been standing since the 13thC, are known as the Binnenhof. Other government buildings and three royal palaces add to the city's grandeur, and there are many fine museums, including the Mauritshuis which houses works by Rubens (see **A-Z**) and Vermeer (see **A-Z**). At Zeestraat 65b you will find the *Panorama Mesdag*, a massive depiction of the village of Scheveningen, finished by Mesdag in 1881 and one of the very few surviving examples of panoramic painting. The three-dimensional effect is quite extraordinary. But The Hague is not all ceremony and art: its parks are excellent, and the miniature city of Madurodam (see **A-Z**) has great appeal.

Hilversum: 30 km southeast of Amsterdam. Pop: 88,000. Hilversum is a pleasant residential city in the heart of the Gooi forest, with many parks designed by W. W. Dudok, and is mainly notable as the centre of the Netherlands' radio and broadcasting services (see **Television & Radio**).

History: Amsterdam derives its name from the dam built over the Amstel river (see **CANALS & RIVERS**) in the 13thC, on the site of what is now Dam Square (see **A-Z**), which led to Amsterdam's growth from a fishing village to a major port. Streets and canals spread out from the dam, gradually and relentlessly pushing back the town's limits until it reached its present proportions. Remains of ancient fortifications which can still be seen today are the Schreierstoren (see **A-Z**) and the Montelbaanstoren on the Oudeschans.

The girdle of main canals (see **CANALS & RIVERS**, **A-Z**) that gives the city so much of its character was developed by the 17thC, when the prosperous times known as the Golden Age saw the building of many splendid merchants' houses. Amsterdam's establishment as a centre of Protestantism in these post-Reformation times did not affect the traditional tolerance of its people. Roman Catholics could always find a place to worship and Jewish immigrants were readily accommodated. The latter's legacy remains to this day, having survived occupation by the Nazis in World War II (see **CHURCHES**, **CITY DISTRICTS**).

Modern Amsterdam is a bustling, cosmopolitan centre which provides everything for the visitor, from high culture to lowlife. The major museums stand comparison with the best in the world, beautiful buildings are to be seen everywhere, the complex of canals is extremely picturesque and the city abounds in cultural events and nightlife.

Houses: Built on wooden stakes over the water, many old city houses tilt forward, possibly because of subsidence or possibly because they were specifically constructed this way to avoid erosion of the façades and gables – so the story goes, anyway. The tall, narrow canal houses with their varied façades and gables (see **A-Z**) are a major attraction for the visitor to Amsterdam. Many date from the 17thC, and recent renovation work has assured their survival in trendier parts of the city such as the Jordaan (see **A-Z**), which had previously been in decline. Continuing Amsterdam's reputation for excellence in architecture, the Amsterdam School (see **Architecture**) designed many bold and imaginative housing schemes in the 1920s and 30s which still seem fresh and innovative today.

IJsselmeer: Formerly the Zuider Zee, a tidal sea which for centuries supported a lucrative fishing industry. The construction (1932) of the Afsluitdijk from Den Oever in Noord-Holland to Zurich in Friesland converted the sea to an inland lake, which was renamed the IJsselmeer. Vast tracts of land were dyked and drained (see **Dykes**), thereby reducing the IJsselmeer in size, and further reclamation is proposed for the 1990s. The N 302 dyke road, which was opened in the mid-1970s, bisected the lake and the southern part was renamed the Markermeer (see **A–Z**). The lack of a troublesome tide makes the IJsselmeer an ideal boating area, and the old fishing ports on the coast are often visited this way (see **EXCURSION 1**). Even inexperienced sailors should find little difficulty in navigating the lake after some basic training.

Jordaan, The: A trendy, lively part of Amsterdam to the west of the Prinsengracht (see **CANALS & RIVERS**) which has undergone a revival in recent years after a period of decline. Once a working-class residential area, it has now become popular with middle-class and artistic members of the community, and bustles with renewed vitality. Its streets and canals are compact and neat, and are all named after plants and flowers. The residents assiduously maintain the area's improved image by planting greenery along the streets and cultivating window boxes. Every day seems to be marked by the opening of a new shop, and the numerous cafés and craft studios contribute greatly to the agreeable atmosphere which prevails here. See **CITY DISTRICTS**, **WALK 1**.

Keukenhof: See **EXCURSION 3**.

Koninklijk Concertgebouw: The world-famous concert hall on Museumplein (see **CITY DISTRICTS**, **SQUARES**) was completed in 1888 to a design by A. L. van Gendt. The resident orchestra built up its reputation under the direction of Willem Kes and Willem Mengelberg over the ensuing decades, and that reputation remains high today. The splendid acoustics in the hall make it a treat for music lovers. Free concerts are held at 1230 on Wed. throughout the year, and the summertime evening concerts are not expensive. Check the press (see **Newspapers**) for details of performances during the season (Sep.-Mar.) and during the

Holland Festival (see **Events**). See OFFICIAL BUILDINGS, THEATRE & CINEMA 1.

Koninklijk Paleis (Royal Palace): The grandeur of the Koninklijk

Paleis belies the fact that when it was built, in the mid-17thC, it was only intended as the Stadhuis or town hall. Such ostentation was only possible in the Golden Age. So magnificent is the building that Louis Napoleon chose it for his palace in 1808. Today the Dutch royal family uses the palace only occasionally and it serves as a museum.
The entrance to the palace is hard to find behind the seven arches embellishing the façade and the story goes that the doorway was made as unobtrusive as possible to protect the Stadhuis from attack. The interiors are works of art in themselves, with their majestic pillars, ornate carvings and lavish decorations and furnishings.
The Royal Palace is conveniently located on Dam Square (see SQUARES, A–Z) in the heart of the city. See MUSEUMS 1, OFFICIAL BUILDINGS, WALK 2.

Leiden: 41 km southwest of Amsterdam. Pop: 104,000. The town's famous university was established in 1575 by William the Silent, Prince of Orange, as a reward to the inhabitants for their resilience during the year-long siege by the Spanish. It was the first university in the Netherlands, and contributed to Leiden's growth as an academic centre (avowedly Protestant, but on the whole tolerant). It was in Leiden that the Nonconformist preacher John Robinson, having been suspended in England in 1604, found the freedom to exercise his Puritan beliefs. He took many followers with him, and in 1620 they became famous as the Pilgrim Fathers when they sailed for America in the *Mayflower* (their leader remaining in Leiden). The Pilgrim Fathers Documents Centre at Boisotkade 2a records the event. There are many other museums in the town, including the Rijksmuseum van Oudheden (archaeological findings from ancient Egypt and the Netherlands) and the Stedelijk Museum de Lakenhal, Oude Singel 28-32 (paintings, ceramics and antique furnishings). Another of Leiden's attractions is the Hortus Botanicus at Rapenburg 73, one of the first botanical gardens in the world.

Schreierstoren

Leidseplein: A busy square, situated on the edge of the ring of main canals, and the hub of Amsterdam's nightlife (see **A-Z**). Among the profusion of cinemas, restaurants and cafés, you will find the Stadsschouwburg (see **THEATRE & CINEMA 1**), the American Hotel (see **MONUMENTS**) and the Melkweg complex (see **DISCOS**). An ice-rink is set up in the centre of the square during the winter. See **SQUARES**.

Maatjes: These are fresh young herrings caught between the months of May and July. At this time of the year they are sold from street stalls, and you will see local people demonstrating the traditional way of eating them – hold them up by the tail, throw back your head and swallow hard!

Madurodam: A miniature city with working models, situated in The Hague (see **A-Z**). Although many of the buildings are replicas of real buildings from various cities, the town as a whole is not based on any one existing place, but gives a general view of Dutch life. All kinds of vehicles move around the tiny streets, and there is even an accident scene. Attention to detail is superb throughout (the scale is 1:25), and Madurodam looks especially attractive illuminated at night. See **CHILDREN**.

Magere Brug: A white, wooden swing bridge over the Amstel river (see **CANALS & RIVERS**) which is still operated by pulleys and is a favourite subject for holiday snaps.

Marken: 20 km northeast of Amsterdam. Pop: 2000. Formerly an isolated fishing community on an island in the Zuider Zee (see **Markermeer**), Marken suffered badly from the enclosure of the sea in 1932 and turned to tourism to replace the lost income. The picturesque tarred houses on stilts and the traditional costumes which are still worn by the inhabitants have proved to be great attractions. Today only a causeway links the island to the mainland, but the proposed reclamation of land from the surrounding sea threatens to incorporate it fully into polder land. However, for the moment, Marken maintains its rather eccentric individuality. See **EXCURSION 1**.

Markermeer: The name given to that part of the IJsselmeer (see **A-Z**) enclosed in 1975 by the N 302 dyke (see **A-Z**) road from Enkhuizen (see **A-Z**) to Lelystad. See **EXCURSION 1**.

Munttoren: Situated on Muntplein (see **SQUARES**), the Munttoren (Mint Tower) was built by Hendrick de Keyser (see **Architecture**) on the remains of an ancient city gate. In 1672, 50 years after its construction, the tower was used as the local mint at a time when the French army was occupying Utrecht (see **A-Z**), which housed the existing mint. It has since retained the name which derives from its function at that time. See **MONUMENTS**.

Music: Whatever your taste in music, you will find something to your liking at any time of the year in one of Amsterdam's numerous venues. On a less formal level, there are also buskers and street entertainers in all the city's major squares during the summer. See **THEATRE & CINEMA 1 & 2**, **Events**, **Koninklijk Concertgebouw**.

Nature: Amsterdam is justifiably proud of its extensive parkland and greenery. Amid all the hustle and bustle of the city you are never far from a quiet park in which to get away from it all. The Amsterdamse Bos (see **PARKS**) to the southeast is a large woodland area which was specially designed to provide employment for the victims of the 1920s depression. For animal lovers, there is Artis Zoo (see **CHILDREN**), which provides a wonderful natural environment for its animals. Outside the city there is a bird sanctuary at Alphen aan de Rijn (see **A-Z**) and an ape sanctuary at Apeldoorn in Gelderland. Texel, an island 85 km north of Amsterdam, is the best location for bird-watching. It can be reached by ferry from Den Helder.

Red-light District: Concentrated in that part of the old town surrounding the northern ends of Oudezijds Voorburgwal and Oudezijds Achterburgwal, the notorious Red-light District exerts a fascination for even the most staid of Amsterdam's visitors. The buildings of genuine historical interest like the Oude Kerk (see **CHURCHES**) and the excellent Amstelkring Museum (see **MUSEUMS 2**) seem incongruous among the gaudy sights of lurid sex shops and prostitutes seated in the windows. The area is known by the locals as the *Walletjes* (Little Walls), and the affectionate name conveys the sense of good-natured wickedness that pervades the district. The atmosphere is a little more intimidating by day as drug addicts and pushers tend to hang around, but when the clubs open at night and the streets become crowded you can wander around quite safely, taking in the remarkable sights. See **CITY DISTRICTS, WALK 4**.

Rembrandt (1606-69): Rembrandt Harmensz van Rijn was born in Leiden (see **A-Z**) and studied painting from an early age. Settling in Amsterdam in 1631, he embarked on an artistic career which was to establish him as the Netherlands' most famous painter, and, in many people's minds, its best. His reputation was established with *The Anatomical Lesson* in 1632 (see **Waag**). In 1642 he produced the famous *Night Watch*, which was not highly regarded at the time, but nowadays is accepted as his masterpiece. It is one of the glories of the Rijksmuseum (see **A-Z**), where many of his paintings and sketches are housed. More of his works can be seen in his former home, Het Rembrandthuis (see **MUSEUMS 3**). Rembrandt died in poverty.

Rembrandtsplein: Situated near the northern reaches of the Amstel river (see **CANALS & RIVERS**) and Muntplein (see **SQUARES**), Rembrandtsplein is one of Amsterdam's lively nightlife (see **A-Z**) centres. A statue of the great painter (see **Rembrandt**) stands in the centre, and restaurants, bars, strip clubs and cinemas border the square, which bustles with noise and activity at night. The most notable building in the vicinity is the incredible Tuschinski Cinema (see **THEATRE & CINEMA 1**). See **SQUARES, WALK 5**.

Rijksmuseum: Designed by P. J. H. Cuypers (see **Architecture**) in the 1880s, this neo-Gothic building did not meet with great favour at the time of its construction. It is colossal and demands a visit of at least several hours to do justice to the magnificent art treasures it contains. Exhibits include ceramics, glassware, silverware, textiles and even dolls' houses, but the main attraction is the collection of paintings, and in particular the works of Rembrandt (see **A-Z**), Franz Hals and Vermeer (see **A-Z**). There are also displays of Asian and Islamic art, 18th and 19thC paintings, and sculpture of all kinds. The ground floor contains historical exhibits relating to the Netherlands dating from medieval times to World War II. See **MUSEUMS 1, WALK 3**.

Rotterdam: 80 km southwest of Amsterdam. Pop: 555,000. Europe's biggest port, Rotterdam sits on a vast estuary formed by the rivers Maas and Rhine. Very few old buildings survived the bombing raids of World

Rijksmuseum

War II and the city has virtually been rebuilt since then, its seafaring heritage having greatly influenced the architecture of the modern buildings. The harbour is one of the busiest in the world and can be seen by boat on a guided tour which will take you right inside the docks. There is a panoramic view of the port from the Euromast, at Parkhaven 20, but this is only for those with a head for heights. The Boymans-van Beuningen Museum at Mathenesserlaan 18-20 has a fine collection of Dutch paintings, including works by Hieronymus Bosch, Pieter Brueghel, Peter Paul Rubens (see **A-Z**) and Rembrandt (see **A-Z**).

Rubens, Sir Peter Paul (1577-1640): A painter born in Siegen in Westphalia where his father was exiled. The bourgeois Rubens family lived there in a state of poverty, but still managed to give their son a good education in Antwerp. From an early age he could speak Flemish, French, German and Latin, and at 14 he began to study painting. In 1600 he travelled round Italy, which greatly influenced his later work and where he met Monteverdi and Galileo. Returning to Antwerp in 1608, he continued his career as a painter of cathedral frescoes, although he was also much valued for his skills as a diplomat. He died leaving over 2000 works, some of which are housed in the Mauritshuis in The Hague (see **A-Z**) and the Boymans-van Beuningen Museum in Rotterdam (see **A-Z**).

Schreierstoren: This ancient monument stands near Centraal station (see **OFFICIAL BUILDINGS**) at the north end of the Geldersekade. It was originally part of the ancient fortifications that protected the city, and once overlooked the sea (before the modern-day expansion of the harbour). Legend has it that this was the spot where the women of Amsterdam gathered to wave tearful farewells to their husbands as they set off on voyages of exploration during the Middle Ages. The name means 'Tower of Tears'. See **MONUMENTS**, **WALK 4**.

Stedelijk Museum: Amsterdam's foremost collection of modern and contemporary art is housed in this neo-Renaissance building, dating from the 1890s, in Museumplein (see **SQUARES**). There are frequent temporary exhibitions, so check in the entrance hall to find out what is currently on offer. Among the permanent exhibits, you will find works by Picasso, Van Gogh, Chagall, Cézanne, Matisse and Monet. The museum also focuses on De Stijl, the group of artists, architects, and designers of the 1920s and 30s whose major figures included Piet Mondrian and Gerrit Rietveld (see **Architecture**). American pop art is also well represented. See **MUSEUMS 1**, **WALK 3**.

Street Numbers: In times gone by houses were not identified by numbers but by the insignia displayed on their façades, often depicting the owner's trade. Many of these can still be seen today. The Amsterdams Historisch Museum (see **MUSEUMS 2**) has a collection of such house heraldries, the oldest of which dates back to 1603 and portrays a milkmaid. This tradition continues today in some quarters: for instance there is a sculpted welding hammer dating from 1973 poised above a welder's door on Oudelbrakstraat. Louis Napoleon introduced street numbers in 1806, and they follow the conventional system of even and odd numbers on opposite sides of the street. In addresses, the number follows the street name.

Tasting Houses: These drinking houses, known as *proeflokaals,* are singular to Amsterdam. Originally they were the sampling houses of the *jenever* distilleries (see **Drinks**), where customers could taste their products before purchasing the bottle of their choice, but now off-sales are prohibited. Pop in and enjoy some of the many varieties of *jenever* on offer. Their décor is usually cheerful but basic, with no tables or chairs.

Tulips: Tulip bulbs were first brought to the Netherlands by sailors returning from Turkey around 1600. The name is thought to originate from the Turkish *tulband,* meaning 'turban'. A chemist named Wulich Kierwertz is credited with installing the first window box containing tulips. Within 50 years the flowers were popular all over the Netherlands and by 1634 tulip bulbs were being quoted on the stock exchange. The business expanded so much over the next few years that bulbs cost as much as f4400 each. In 1637 the government stepped in and prices dropped, causing many investors to go bankrupt (including the famous painter Jan Van Goyen). Today the main tulip-growing areas lie to the southwest of Amsterdam. See **EXCURSION 3**, **Best Buys**, **Drijvende Bloemenmarkt**, **Haarlem**.

Utrecht: 38 km southeast of Amsterdam. Pop: 230,000. This city, the fourth-largest in the Netherlands, played a major role in the ecclesiastical history of the country. Its surviving religious buildings constitute the city's main attractions (there are numerous churches and convents, many of great antiquity) as much of the modern city is rather unprepossessing. The Domtoren (Cathedral tower) on Domplein is the most outstanding building in old Utrecht and dates from the 13thC. Climb it for excellent views of the city. Among the few museums to visit is the Music Box and Barrel Organ Museum at Achter de Dom 12, which is a real curiosity.

Van Gogh Museum: Opened in 1973, this modern building was designed by Gerrit Rietveld (see **Architecture**) and houses the private collection of Theo Van Gogh, brother of the great and troubled artist, Vincent. The museum sets out to give a complete insight into the life and character of the man as well as his work. Letters and documents are exhibited, as well as articles written about Van Gogh and examples of his influence on his contemporaries and on the art world in general. However, the central core of the collection consists of over 200 paintings and 500 drawings by Vincent himself. See MUSEUMS 1, WALK 3.

Vermeer, Jan (1632-75): A native of Delft (see **A-Z**) and a contemporary of Rembrandt (see **A-Z**), Vermeer is recognized now, if not during his own lifetime, as one of the great painters of the Golden Age. Few details about his life are known, perhaps because his Catholicism required him to maintain a low profile.
Precision and detail are the two main hallmarks of his work. His output was not prodigious, but some of his most notable paintings can be seen in the Rijksmuseum (see **A-Z**), and in the Mauritshuis in The Hague (see **A-Z**).

Volendam: 18 km northeast of Amsterdam. Pop: 17,000. Volendam is a small port on the Markermeer (see **A-Z**) which, like so many others in the area, had to turn to tourism to replace the income once generated by fishing that was lost by the enclosure of the Zuider Zee (see **IJsselmeer**). Visitors now flock to see the harbour and the local inhabitants bedecked in their colourful traditional costumes. See EXCURSION 1.

Vondelpark: In the 1960s Amsterdam's main city-centre park attracted droves of flower people and hippies. Today it retains some of the same free-and-easy atmosphere. All kinds of open-air entertainments go on here during the summer, both theatrical and musical, impromptu and prearranged. Its sports facilities are also good, and the park houses the interesting Nederlands Filmmuseum (see MUSEUMS 3). See PARKS.

Waag: Situated in Nieuwmarkt, the Waag (weigh house) is a remnant of the old city wall and has many interesting corners to explore. It was once used by various local guilds: the surgeons' guild dissected the bodies of executed criminals here, as Rembrandt's (see **A-Z**) famous painting *The Anatomical Lesson* records. The Waag formerly housed the Amsterdams Historisch and Joods Historisch museums (see **MUSEUMS 2**).

Zaandam: See **EXCURSION 2**.

Zaanse Schans: A reconstruction of a 17th-18thC windmill village, built in 1960 and located outside Zaandam (see **EXCURSION 2**). Here you can explore various antiquities museums, visit old-style houses and shops, and watch craftsmen working at their various trades. The numerous windmills contribute to the town's picturesque appeal. See **EXCURSION 2**.

Zandvoort: 30 km west of Amsterdam. Pop: 16,000. A seaside resort with miles of beaches fringed by cafés and restaurants. To the north is the motor-racing circuit which hosts the Dutch Formula One Grand Prix. See **EXCURSION 2**.

Zuider Zee: See **IJsselmeer, Markermeer**.

Accidents & Breakdowns: If you are involved in a motoring accident follow the normal procedure of exchanging names, addresses and insurance details with the other party, while saying nothing that could be considered an admission of liability. If the accident is serious, tel: 0611 for the emergency services.

In the event of a breakdown, move your car off the road (if possible) and place a hazard warning triangle an adequate distance behind the vehicle. AA and RAC members may use the services of their Dutch equivalent, the Dutch Automobile Association Emergency Service (ANWB), tel: 020-6268251. Temporary membership costs very little. See **Consulates**, **Driving**.

Accommodation: Amsterdam is well provided with hotels of all categories, from the most basic to the most luxurious. A double room can cost as little as f60 or as much as f475 per night. As you would expect, comfort and facilities provided are reflected in the price, so it is advisable to look at the room before registering, especially in cheaper hotels. The VVV (see **Tourist Information**) will book accommodation for a fee of f3.50, but postal requests for this service are not accepted. For accommodation outside the city, the first night must be paid for in advance at the VVV office. See **Camping & Caravanning**, **Youth Hostels**.

Airport: Schiphol, 15 km southwest of Amsterdam on the A 10 and A 9 motorways, is one of the world's most popular airports, as numerous consumer surveys prove. It handles flights to and from all the major international destinations. Buses, trains and the Metro provide regular services between here and Centraal station (see **OFFICIAL BUILDINGS**). There are also taxi ranks. The journey takes about 15 min.

Baby-sitters: Your hotel will probably be able to arrange a baby-sitter for you. Rates are approximately f4 per hr before 2400, f5 per hr 2400-0300, and f10 per hr after 0300. Also tel: 6231708 between 1730 and 1900 for the Student Baby-sitting Service. See **CHILDREN**, **Children**.

Banks: See **Currency**, **Money**, **Opening Times**.

Best Buys: Flowers can vary in price according to the season, but they are always remarkably cheap. House plants are also very good value. The Floating Flower Market (see **Drijvende Bloemenmarkt**) offers a wide choice (see **Tulips**). You are allowed to bring up to 2 kg of bulbs or tubers, five plants or cuttings, five packets of seeds and one small bunch of flowers into Britain. Chinaware is also a good buy. There is a great deal of imitation Delft china around so be careful. The real thing is more expensive, but still cheaper than outside the Netherlands (see **Delft**). Amsterdam is also famous for diamonds (see **A-Z**), which are less expensive here than just about anywhere else in the world. Plain and painted wooden clogs are sold in many gift shops and are a popular present. Cigars are so inexpensive that they make ideal gifts for smokers, and hand-rolling tobacco is also a good buy (see **SHOPPING 4**). Other popular souvenirs include dolls in traditional costume and model windmills. See **SHOPPING 1-4**, **Markets**, **Shopping**.

Bicycle Hire: Hire shops are plentiful, especially near the railway stations. The daily rate is approximately f7, the weekly rate approximately f28. A deposit of f100-f200 is usually required. You will lose this deposit if the bike is stolen; theft is very common, so beware. Yellow Bike offers 3.5 hr guided cycling tours round the city starting at Beurs van Berlage, Damrak 247, with departures at 0900, 1300 and 1900. For further information contact them at Nieuwezijds Voorburgwal 66, 1012 SC Amsterdam, tel: 206940. See **Bicycles**.

Boat Hire: Sailing boats, complete with skipper, can be hired from De Ruijterkade behind Centraal station (see **OFFICIAL BUILDINGS**), and elsewhere, at a cost of approximately f75 per hr. A four-person motorboat costs about f37.50 per hr. The small towns along the coast of the Markermeer and IJsselmeer (see **A-Z**) provide excellent mooring facilities. All boats for hire are insured, but a hefty deposit will be required.

Budget:

Breakfast	f10-f20
Lunch	f20-f30
Beer	f2-f3
Soft drink	f2-f3
Museumcard	f30 (valid one year: available from VVV – see **Tourist Information**)
Bus & tram ticket	f8.65 (day), f25 (week)
Theatre ticket	f10-f20

Buses: A number of bus companies provide services to all parts of the city. They operate on the *strippenkaart* fare system (see **Transport**), although daily or weekly tickets, which can be purchased from the VVV (see **Tourist Information**), are more economical if you intend to use public transport regularly. External coach routes also link Amsterdam with other parts of the Netherlands and beyond. See **Tours & Excursions**.

Cameras & Photography: Flash photography is not permitted in some museums and churches; always enquire beforehand. There are shops catering for all photographic requirements, but film is expensive so bring a good supply with you.

Camping & Caravanning: Amsterdam has six main camping sites of a high standard. Advance booking is usually advisable. They charge approximately f3.50-f10 per night per person (car included). Tent hire starts from as little as f1. See **PARKS**.

Canal Bike Hire: A four-person canal bike (pedalo) costs approximately f27.50 per hr, a two-person bike f18.50 per hr. You can hire them at the Singelgracht, near Leidseplein, and the Prinsengracht, at Westermarkt.

Car Hire: All the major international companies are represented in the Netherlands and can be found at Schiphol (see **Airport**). Few firms have offices in the centre of Amsterdam, but those which do are listed in the *Yellow Pages* under 'Autoverhuur'. Hiring a car is only really worthwhile for touring outside the city. Rates are approximately f60-f120 per day.

Chemists: These follow normal opening times (see **A-Z**) Mon.-Fri. and a rota system for evenings and weekends. For the address of the nearest open pharmacy, tel: 132855. See **Health**.

Children: Youngsters are well catered for in Amsterdam. There is no shortage of museums, theatres and parks providing facilities and entertainment for their enjoyment. Families are welcome in most cafés, bars and restaurants, but if in doubt check beforehand. See CHILDREN, **Baby-sitters**.

Climate: The weather in the Netherlands is typical of northwestern European countries – generally mild in winter and cool in summer, but unpredictable at all times. July and Aug. are normally the warmest months (approximately 20°C), but spring is usually drier than summer.

Complaints: If you have been overcharged, or find that prices do not correspond to those displayed, ask to see the owner or manager of the premises. If you are still not satisfied, then you can report the establishment to the VVV (see **Tourist Information**) or the police (see **A-Z**), but you will find that just threatening this course of action is usually sufficient.

Consulates:
UK – Koningslaan 44, Amsterdam, tel: 6764343.
Republic of Ireland – Willemskade 23, Rotterdam, tel: 010-143322.
Australia – Koninginnegracht 23, The Hague, tel: 070-630983.
Canada – Sophialaan 7, The Hague, tel: 070-614111.
New Zealand – Mauritskade 25, The Hague, tel: 070-469324.
USA – Museumplein 19, Amsterdam, tel: 6790321/6717030.

Conversion Chart:

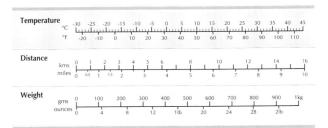

Credit Cards: See **Money**.

Crime & Theft: Amsterdam is a reasonably safe city, but there are still risks. Beware of pickpockets at all times and keep an eye on your bicycle as theft is very common. Keep to busy well-lit streets at night, or travel by taxi (see **A-Z**).
The Red-light District (see **A-Z**) actually has a more intimidating atmosphere during the daylight hours as drug addicts and pushers are a common sight, but by and large they will not bother you if you ignore them.
Should you run into trouble you will find the police headquarters at Elandsgracht 117, tel: 5599111, and there are police services for overseas visitors at Waterlooplein 9, tel: 5593395 (0900-1500 Mon.-Wed. & Fri.). See **Consulates**, **Emergency Numbers**, **Insurance**, **Police**.

Currency: The guilder is the national monetary unit of the Netherlands (abbreviated as Dfl, Fl or f). There are 100 cents (ct) to the guilder. Coins in circulation are worth 5ct, 10ct, 25ct, f1, f2.50 and f5. Notes are in denominations of f5, f10, f25, f50, f100 and f1000. See **Money**.

Customs Allowances:

Duty Paid Into:	Cigarettes	*or*	Cigars	*or*	Tobacco	Spirits	Wine
EC	300		75		400 g	1.5 *l*	5 *l*
UK	300		75		400 g	1.5 *l*	5 *l*

Disabled People: Facilities for the disabled are fairly good throughout the Netherlands, although the old buildings and narrow streets obviously create difficulties. The Netherlands Board of Tourism, 25-28 Buckingham Gate, London SW1E 6LD, can provide a list of hotels, restaurants and places of interest with suitable facilities. See **Health**, **Insurance**.

Drinks: The most popular alcoholic drink in Holland is beer, served German-style with a large frothy head. But for a taste of traditional Dutch spirits try a glass of *jenever* (see **Tasting Houses**), a drink which gave its name to gin, but is weaker and tastes slightly different to the British version. Both young and old varieties are available, as are blackcurrant (*bessenjenever*) and lemon (*citroenjenever*) flavours, as well as *bittertje*, the Dutch version of pink gin. There is also the famous eggy, yellow advocaat, which is the main constituent of a snowball cocktail. Imported wines and liqueurs tend to be more expensive. There are no licensing restrictions in Amsterdam, so cafés and bars set their own opening times.
Popular non-alcoholic drinks include coffee (usually excellent), tea (to a lesser extent) and the usual range of soft and fizzy drinks, as well as fruit juices.

Driving: If you are taking your car to the Netherlands you will need a valid national driving licence, your car registration papers and a national identity sign on the vehicle. Hiring a car just for getting about the city is not advisable due to traffic congestion and parking difficulties (see **Parking**).

Remember to drive on the right and overtake on the left. Give way to trams, pedestrians at crossings and traffic approaching from the right. Observe the speed restrictions (generally 50 kph in built-up areas, 80 kph on main roads, 120 kph on motorways, unless otherwise indicated). Be particularly vigilant in looking out for cyclists: cars turning right must give way to cyclists continuing straight on. The wearing of seat belts is compulsory. See **Accidents & Breakdowns**, **Car Hire**, **Parking**, **Petrol**.

Drugs: Contrary to many people's expectations, drugs are not legal in Amsterdam. In practice, however, the authorities generally turn a blind eye to the sale, possession and consumption of small amounts of cannabis. It is readily obtainable in many coffee shops. Hard drugs such as cocaine and heroin are quite another matter, and if you are caught in possession of these you could face a prison sentence. It is not uncommon to see addicts and dealers on the streets. Because of Amsterdam's reputation as a drugs centre, customs officials are extremely vigilant, so it is foolish to try to get the better of them. The Drugs Advice Centre is situated at Keizersgracht 812 (1300-1500 Mon.-Fri.). See **Emergency Numbers**.

Eating Out: Although not renowned as a gourmet's paradise, Amsterdam does have a wide range of restaurants to suit all tastes and pockets. Many are clustered round Leidseplein (see **A-Z**) and Rembrandtsplein (see **A-Z**). As a consequence of the Netherlands' imperial past there are numerous Indonesian and Surinamese restaurants, while other ethnic cuisines available include Cantonese, Japanese, Indian, Creole, Pakistani and Greek. Look out for the Tourist Menu sign in restaurant windows; it indicates that inexpensive three-course set meals are available. The familiar international fast-food chains are all represented.

Leidseplein

In the **RESTAURANTS** topic section a three-course meal (not including wine) in an inexpensive restaurant could come to less than f25 a head; f25-f50 can be considered moderate; expensive establishments will set you back upwards of f50. See **RESTAURANTS 1-3**, **Food**.

Electricity: 220 volts. Two-pin plugs are used and adaptors can be purchased in electrical shops in Britain and the Netherlands.

Emergency Numbers:

Police, fire brigade, ambulance   0611
Central Medical Service   6642111
Social services   6161666
Drugs helpline   6948460

Events:

February: The Carnival, a parade from the Oosterdok to Rembrandtsplein (see **A-Z**), fancy dress, dancing, lots of beer and nonstop music in the streets.
March: The Koninklijk Concertgebouw orchestra's (see **A-Z**) Easter programme; Nieuwe Kerk antique fair.
April: Electrische Museumtramlijn – rides from Karperweg 44 to the Amsterdamse Bos (see **PARKS**) on vintage trams (until Oct.); *30:* Queen's

Day, public holiday with street musicians, stalls and events.
May: Kunst RAI – art fair at the exhibition hall (see **OFFICIAL BUILDINGS**);
15: Antiques market on Beursplein (until Sep.).
June: Holland Festival – art exhibitions, dance, music and theatre.
July-August: Summer programmes in many theatres.
August: Uitmarkt – start of the cultural season.
September: Jordaan Festival; *1st Sat.:* Flower parade from Aalsmeer
(see **A-Z**) to Amsterdam.

October: Autumn opening and art exhibition in the Koninklijk Paleis (see **A-Z**).
25 November: St. Nicolaas parade (see CHURCHES).

Gambling: The Casino Amsterdam at the Hilton Hotel, Apollolaan 138 (1400-0300, day ticket f7.50) features roulette, blackjack and gaming machines. Smart attire is necessary. Amusement arcades are also to be found in the main tourist areas such as Damrak, Rembrandtsplein, Muntplein and Leidseplein.

Health: The Netherlands offers a high standard of medical care. The Academisch Medisch Centrum at Meibergdreef 9 is one of the leading hospitals in Amsterdam, and there are casualty clinics offering first-aid services at Oosterparkstraat 179, de Boelelaan 1117 and Oudezijds Voorburgwal 127. Round-the-clock information on dental and medical care is available from the Central Medical Service (see **Emergency Numbers**). See **Chemists**, **Disabled People**, **Insurance**.

Insurance: You should take out travel insurance covering you against theft and loss of property and money, as well as medical expenses, for the duration of your stay. Your travel agent should be able to recommend a suitable policy for you. See **Crime & Theft**, **Driving**, **Health**.

Laundries: Launderettes are known as *wasserij* and dry-cleaners as *stomerij.* There are Launderettes at Rozengracht 59, Herenstraat 24 and Oude Doelenstraat 12; and that at Warmoesstraat 30 is open 24 hr.

Lost Property Offices:
Police lost property office – Waterlooplein 11, tel: 5599111 (1100-1530 Mon.-Fri.).
Buses & trams – Prins Hendrikkade 108, tel: 5514911 (0830-1530 Mon.-Fri.).
Trains – tel: 5578544 (0700-2200 Mon.-Sat.).
Taxis – tel: 777777.
Schiphol airport – tel: 491433.

Markets: Amsterdam has several lively and colourful street markets of all kinds where bargains are to be had for locals and visitors alike. For general goods, try the Flea Market (see A-Z), Westerstraat, Albert Cuypstraat or Nieuwmarkt (see **WALK 4**). Antique lovers will enjoy the markets at Looiersgracht 38 and Elandsgracht 109, while bookworms should investigate Oudemanhuispoort. See **CHURCHES**, **Drijvende Bloemenmarkt**.

Metro: The underground system in Amsterdam is primarily a suburban commuter service, but it does provide an alternative means of reaching the Jewish Quarter (see **CITY DISTRICTS**). Payment is by the *strippenkaart* system (see **Transport**).

Money: Banks offer all the usual facilities. Centraal station (see **OFFICIAL BUILDINGS**) has a branch of the GWK (Grenwisselkantoor) which is open 0700-2245 daily. There are also many exchange kiosks on the main streets in the city centre which are open conveniently long hours, but offer less favourable terms. Most larger stores, restaurants and hotels accept all the major credit cards, though not all hotels accept traveller's cheques in payment. Traveller's cheques can be readily exchanged at banks and *bureaux de change*. See **Crime & Theft**, **Currency**.

Newspapers: The Dutch national dailies include *De Telegraaf*, *Het Parool* and *De Volkskrant*. The *Holland Herald* is published monthly in English and features news and listings. The major international newspapers and periodicals are widely available, and British papers appear on the day of publication. See **What's On**.

Nightlife: Most Amsterdammers tend to eat early. Dinner at home is usually over by 1930, leaving the evening free for going to the theatre or cinema, or having a few drinks. Bars close around midnight or 0100, when business starts to pick up in the discos. The Red-light District (see A-Z), with its peep-shows, sex shops and seedy clubs, is one of the busiest nightlife areas. 'Topless' bars can be found on Thorbeckeplein. See **CAFÉS**, **DISCOS**, **MODERN BARS**, **THEATRE & CINEMA 1 & 2**, **Gambling**.

Opening Times: These inevitably vary, but generally:
Banks – 0900-1600 Mon.-Wed. & Fri., 0900-1900 Thu.
Post offices – 0830-1800 Mon.-Wed. & Fri., 0830-2030 Thu., 0900-1200 Sat.
VVV (Tourist Information Service) – 0900-1900 (Nov.-Mar.); 0845-2300 Mon.-Sat., 1000-1730 Sun. (April-Oct.).
Shops – 1300-1800 Mon., 0900-1800 Tue., Wed. & Fri., 0900-2100 Thu., 0900-1700 Sat.

Orientation: The centre of Amsterdam is bounded to the north by Centraal station (see **OFFICIAL BUILDINGS**), where many tram and bus routes terminate. The main thoroughfares of Nieuwezijds Voorburgwal and Damrak run south from here through Dam Square (see **SQUARES**), Damrak becoming Rokin at this point. The southern ends of these streets lie in Spui and Muntplein (see **SQUARES**). To the east are the Red-light District (see **A-Z**), the old town and the Jewish Quarter (see **CITY DISTRICTS**), which are intersected by Oudezijds Voorburgwal, Oudezijds Achterburgwal, Geldersekade, Kloveniersburgwal and Oudeschans (all running roughly north to south). The main canals (see **CANALS & RIVERS**) form two-thirds of a horseshoe shape, enclosing these areas on their western and southern sides. The Jordaan (see **A-Z**) lies further to the west on the other side of the canals, while the Museumplein district (see **CITY DISTRICTS**, **SQUARES**) and the fashionable Old South are to the south of the city centre, also across the canals.

Parking: Searching for a parking space in Amsterdam can be a frustrating experience. Metered bays (which charge reasonable rates) are to be found on many of the side streets, but they are usually occupied from early in the morning and double parking is quite common. Illegally parked cars run the risk of being towed away and a hefty fine is payable for recovery. There are multistorey car parks on Marnixstraat near the police station, at Centraal station and by the Bÿenkorff. See **Driving**.

Passports & Customs: For visits of up to three months, nationals from European Community countries, North America, Australia and New Zealand require only a valid passport to enter the Netherlands. However, other nationals may in addition require a visa. See **Customs Allowances**.

Pedalos: See **Canal Bike Hire**.

Petrol: There are fewer places to buy petrol in Amsterdam than in many other major cities, but you will find numerous modern service stations outside the city. Prices do not vary significantly from the rest of western Europe. See **Driving**.

Police: Although the police are armed and have adopted a higher profile in recent years (in order to clamp down on the drug problem), they generally have a laid-back attitude and are extremely approachable. See **Crime & Theft**, **Emergency Numbers**.

Post Offices: The main post office is now at Singel 250 (see OFFICIAL BUILDINGS), and there are smaller branches throughout the city. You can also buy stamps at postcard kiosks and from slot machines. Parcels are handled by the Postkantoor which is located at Oosterdok 3-5. See **Opening Times**.

Public Holidays: 1 Jan.; Easter Mon.; 30 April (Queen's Day); Ascension Day (usually in early May); Whit Mon. (mid-May); 25-26 Dec.

Rabies: Still exists here as in other parts of the Continent. As a precaution have all animal bites seen to immediately by a doctor.

Railways: A modern, efficient railway system links Amsterdam to all parts of the Netherlands and the rest of the Continent. Services within the city largely cater for suburban travel (see **Metro**). Ticket prices are moderate, and reduced fares are available for regular travellers. Centraal station (see **OFFICIAL BUILDINGS**) is Amsterdam's main railway station.

Religious Services:
Reformed churches:

Westerkerk, Prinsengracht 281 (1030).
Oude Kerk, Oudekerksplein 23 (1100).
Engelse Kerk, Begijnhof 48 (1030, in English).
Church of England, Groenburgwal 42 (1030).

Roman Catholic:

Begijnhofkerk, Begijnhof 29 (1200, in English).
De Papegaai, Kalverstraat 58 (0900, 1045, 1215).
St. Nicolaaskerk, Prins Hendrikkade 73 (1100).

Shopping: Some of the main shopping areas are:
Kalverstraat – a pedestrianized street with a variety of shops of all sizes.
Pieter Cornelisz Hooftstraat/Beethovenstraat/Van Baerlestraat – up-market shops selling designer clothes and quality goods.
Runstraat/Huidenstraat – unusual small boutiques and gift shops.
Spiegelgracht/Nieuwe Spiegelstraat – works of art, antiques, gifts.
See **SHOPPING 1-4**, **Best Buys**, **Markets**, **Opening Times**.

Smoking: Smoking is prohibited in public buildings as well as on a lot of business premises, and on trams and buses. However, the anti-smoking lobby has yet to make any impact at all on Amsterdam's nightlife. Hardly any restaurants provide no-smoking areas.

Sports: Amsterdam has all the facilities for participatory sports that you would expect in a major city. Cycling (see **Bicycles**), ice-skating (see **Leidseplein**) and sailing (see **Boat Hire**) are particularly associated with the Netherlands. For those who prefer to spectate, there is motor-racing at Zandvoort (see **A-Z**) or football just about anywhere. The biggest local team is the famous Ajax Amsterdam, whose stadium is in the east of the city at Middenweg 401. The ground is small so tickets for important matches must be reserved well in advance. See **PARKS**.

Taxis: You cannot hail taxis in the street, but there are many taxi ranks near railway stations and in busy public areas. Tel: 777777 to order a cab – the service is usually quick and efficient, but rather expensive. A service charge is included in the metered fare, but it is customary to add a small tip (see **Tipping**).

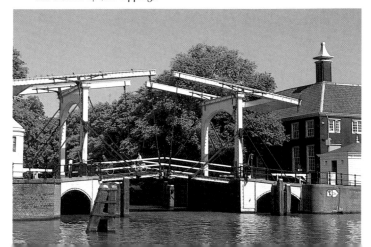

Telephones & Telegrams: There is no shortage of modern, well-maintained telephone boxes. They take 25ct and f1 coins, and most display a guide in English explaining how to operate them. Some telephones operate on a card system. These cards are available at post offices (see **A-Z**) and newsagents. Many cafés and hotels have older telephone boxes which take only 25ct coins. The Telehuis at Raadhuisstraat 48 is open 24 hr for long-distance calls, telegrams, telexes and faxes. Payment is made at the desk after the call is completed. To telephone abroad, dial 09, followed by the appropriate international code (e.g. UK 44, USA 1) when you hear a change in the dialling tone. Then dial the area code (without the initial 0) and the rest of the number.

Television & Radio: The three Hilversum (see **A-Z**) radio stations broadcast a variety of different music programmes, and there are three Dutch television channels which all show undubbed American and British films and series. French films are also often broadcast. British and Continental television and radio stations are easily received with good equipment. Some areas also have cable TV.

Time Difference: Central European Time, which is followed in the Netherlands during the winter months, is ahead of Greenwich Mean Time by 1 hr. Clocks are put forward by 1 hr in summer. Therefore, Amsterdam is always 1 hr ahead of the UK and 6 hr ahead of the east coast of the USA.

Tipping: A service charge is normally included in hotel and restaurant bills, but it is customary also to leave a few coins (f3-f5). Hotel porters expect f2 per bag, while tour guides and taxi drivers expect 5-10% of the fare.

Toilets: Unfortunately these are few and far between, but the standard of cleanliness is high and there are normally facilities for the disabled. Some have an attendant (who may expect a tip), but otherwise public toilets are generally free. *Heren* for men and *Damen* for women.

TOU

A–Z

Tourist Information: The Netherlands Tourist Information Service is known as the VVV (pronounced Vay-Vay-Vay), and their offices bear this logo in blue. In Amsterdam you will find them at Stationsplein 10 and Leidsestraat 106, tel: 020-6266444. As well as providing general information, the VVV will exchange currency, book hotels (for a small fee), issue Museumcards (see **Budget**) and organize excursions, car rental, etc. Their offices are generally busy so expect queues. See **Opening Times**.

Tours & Excursions: Amsterdam, known as the Venice of the North, actually has more canals than Venice and is best seen by boat. There are many tours to choose from, each offering basically the same service, so just opt for the most convenient. Embarkation points are on Prins Hendrikkade, Rokin and Damrak. Boat trips usually last 1 hr and depart every 15 min. More luxurious (and more expensive) dinner cruises, lasting 3 or 4 hr, are available in the evenings. City coach tours are also popular. For example, you can enjoy a 3 hr trip round Dam Square (see **A-Z**), some of the famous bridges, the Rijksmuseum (see **A-Z**) and a diamond (see **A-Z**) factory. There are also specialist tours of museums, diamond factories and other sights of particular interest. A recently-introduced service is the Museum Boat, which departs daily from the Noord-Zuid Hollands Koffie Huis near Centraal station (see **OFFICIAL BUILDINGS**) at 0930, and visits nine main museums (costs f7.50). Company representatives tout for business along the busy thoroughfares like Damrak, offering inexpensive coach trips to major cities such as The Hague (see **A-Z**), Rotterdam (see **A-Z**) and Utrecht (see **A-Z**), and other attractions such as the tulip fields (see **EXCURSION 3**) or the windmill country (see **EXCURSION 2**).

Trams: Most of the centre of Amsterdam, and some areas further afield, are served by trams. They are one of the city's most distinctive sights, and a fast and convenient method of getting around. Payment is by the *strippenkaart* fare system (see **Transport**).

Transport: Buses, trams and the Metro use a fare system known as *strippenkaart*. These tickets can be bought in advance at post offices,

railway stations, newsagents and tobacconists, and consist of two, three, 10 or 15 strips which the passenger must cancel according to the number of fare zones included in the journey (two strips for one zone, three strips for two zones, etc.). Ticket inspections are frequent and fines are stiff. More economical daily or weekly tickets which allow unlimited travel are available from the transport office on Stationsplein (f9.50 and f31.50 respectively). See **Airport**, **Buses**, **Metro**, **Railways**, **Taxis**, **Trams**.

Traveller's Cheques: See **Money**.

What's On: The best way to keep up with the latest happenings is to buy the listings periodical *Amsterdam This Week*, published by the VVV (see **Tourist Information**). See **Events**, **Newspapers**.

Youth Hostels: To stay in youth hostels in the Netherlands you must possess an international YH card. If you do not already have one, it can be obtained from Nederlandse Jeugdherberg, Prof. Tulpplein 4, 1018 GX Amsterdam, tel: 6264433. The charge is f35. Youth hostels cost approximately f18 per night, including breakfast.

This book was produced using QuarkXPress™ and Adobe
Illustrator 88™ on Apple Macintosh™ computers and output to
separated film on a Linotronic™ 300 Imagesetter

Text: Elizabeth Claridge
Photography: Phil Springthorpe
Electronic Cartography: Susan Harvey Design

First published 1990
Second edition 1992
Copyright © HarperCollins Publishers
Published by HarperCollins Publishers
Printed by HarperCollins Manufacturing, Glasgow
ISBN 0 00 470021-X